REMEMBER
THE VINE

A story about the value of time in growing and harvesting capital.

Third Edition

An Investment Novel by
Samuel P. Edwards

Dedication

Dedicated to Jane Myers who assisted in the development of the first edition published in 1990. And to the past employees of Beacon Investment Company.

Cover art: Acrylic on canvas still life,
"The Vine", by Samuel P. Edwards

Table of Contents

The 25-Year Vision

Chapter 1
The Wedding Day

Julie opened one eye slowly and then the other. Sunshine! The weather forecast on the eleven o'clock news the night before had predicted a sixty per cent chance of rain today, and she and Paul didn't want rain on their wedding day if they could have it any other way. They knew they were taking a risk, planning an outdoor wedding in May in Michigan.

The sunny day certainly seemed like a good omen. Looking out the window of her old bedroom, the one she'd looked out so many times as a child, she felt they were on the threshold of a great adventure, one that like all great adventures was both unsettling yet exciting.

She and Paul were plunging headlong into their new life. They weren't even taking time for a honeymoon because they wanted to complete their job interviews, find out what city they'd be living in, look for an apartment.

They hoped they'd have a home of their own before long. Paul's grandfather was a very wealthy man, a man highly respected among his peers. As an investor, teacher and contributor to prestigious technical journals over many years, he had established an international reputation for his expertise and his generosity in sharing his ideas and his wealth with others. An avid playgoer, he kept a penthouse in New York in addition to his lovely old home in Saginaw where he'd lived so many years with Paul's grandmother and raised a family. Paul was his firstborn grandchild and the first to get married. He'd hinted to them that he was going to give them a very valuable wedding gift when they'd last seen him at the family gathering he'd hosted at his ocean-side villa in the Bahamas. They hoped it might be the kind of sizable down payment it took to purchase a nice home these days.

He'd flown the whole family down to the Caribbean for the Christmas holidays and paid for everything. He was one of the most generous men they'd ever met. It seemed he enjoyed sharing his money with others. He'd established an endowed scholarship fund at his college with a gift of $2 million, and he was developing a plan to send hundreds of academically gifted students from inner city high schools to college. He repeatedly extolled the virtues of education. Without the engineering training he'd received in the 1930s on a scholarship program, he said, he never could have developed the electroplating process that had eventually turned him into a millionaire many times over.

He felt strongly that other young people should have the same educational opportunities he'd had.

He was going to attend the wedding, of course, and promised to present them with their gift on their wedding day. It made the prospect of the wonderful day ahead all the more exciting.

Chapter 2

A Wedding Gift From Grandfather

Paul slipped the white envelope into the inside pocket of his tuxedo, and gave his grandfather a hug. If there were ever a moment when he'd feel happier, he couldn't imagine it. The most wonderful woman in the world, the lovely Julie by his side, was now his wife --his wife! All the people he cared most about in the world were with them, the sun was shining brightly, the music was playing, the champagne fountains were bubbling, everyone was eating and talking and having a great time! He felt blessed in every way.

"Thank you, Grandpa," he said. "I love you."

"I love you, too, Paul," his grandfather said. "I wish you both as much happiness and satisfaction as I have found in my life. Only you and Julie can make your dreams come true. But I know that you have the maturity and the desire to succeed and the willingness to work hard to make your dreams a reality.

"My gift to you, I hope, will show you the way toward another essential ingredient, the ability to use those advantages wisely, to remember the fundamental principles that cannot be violated if one is to find true and lasting happiness.

"Open my gift in the quiet of your own togetherness --not now. This is a moment for reveling in the promises you have made today to one another, and for celebrating the promise of the future. Only remember that as long as I am alive, I am here to help you. There is much that you must learn for yourself, but sometimes a person who has been down the path before you can offer valuable insights to help you make the choices that must be made. Having choices and making choices is what my success has been all about, and having choices and making choices will determine your future as well."

The music stopped as all heads turned toward the band and the microphone, where Paul's college roommate and best man, Henry Stafford, was holding his champagne glass aloft. "A toast to the bride and groom, a toast to Julie and Paul! May they dwell in the peace of contentment and shared commitment, in the kindness of respect and understanding. in the richness of love, and the wealth of friendship. May they be forever as happy as they are today."

Paul wrapped his free arm around his bride and gave her a long kiss. Everyone cheered and brought their glasses to their lips, the music played. and his grandfather smiled. It was a wonderful day.

Chapter 3

An Unexpected Journey

At their breakfast table in the hotel the next morning Paul pulled his grandfather's envelope out of his pocket. He and Julie had decided to wait to open it giving the edge of anticipation to what they knew would be an important moment. His grandfather's gift.

It had special meaning, not only because of what it might mean to their marriage and their future, but because of what Grandfather represented to Paul. He was love and wisdom, a warm heart. Some of Paul's earliest memories were of his grandfather patiently pitching a softball to him on a Sunday afternoon while he developed the coordination to swing a bat. Paul couldn't have been more than four or five years old at the time. "Try it again Paul," he'd say. "You can do it!"

"I wanted you to open the envelope," Paul said, handing it to Julie. It was their future in the envelope, after all.

"It's a letter, Paul," Julie said with surprise, "and two airline tickets! And three other sealed envelopes marked 1, 2 and 3! 'Dear Paul and Julie....' OH, you read it Paul, you should be the one to read it." She handed the letter back across the table, and Paul began reading it to Julie, softly, not sure of what he was going to find from one line to the next.

"Dear Paul and Julie'" he began again, "I know this letter will be a surprise to you, and that you probably expected a more customary gift than two plane tickets to a place you didn't know you wanted to go. I could have given you money, but I am certain that cash is not the most valuable gift I could give to you today. By the time you have completed the important journey upon which you are about to embark, I believe you will agree.

For most people, financial security is an important contributor to happiness, not only because of what money can buy but, more importantly, because of what money makes possible. Money provides options, the chance to make choices about how and where you want to live your life. And those choices are what freedom is all about.

But just getting money is not the key to insuring this freedom, this wonderful freedom that we as Americans cherish so highly. Over the centuries, fortunes have been won and lost by people who never obtained financial security or real happiness.

"The key to the financial security and happiness I so fondly desire for you, and know that you desire for yourselves, stems from certain principles, principles known to many but understood and applied by only a few. It is that understanding I wish to give to you.

"Paul, remember the book that we read together when you were very young, the book about the Swiss Family Robinson that you loved so much as a little boy? Well, it is in the Robinson's homeland, Switzerland, that these principles will be explained to you. The principles of good living are universal. All the world's great religions, as you know, share many of the same precepts, which apply to family life, business, investing, to every facet of life. But truly understanding those precepts, knowing how to interpret them and make them your own, and knowing how to impart them to others, requires a special wisdom. The man who will meet you at the airport in Geneva is one of those men.

"He is a friend of mine from many years ago, a Swiss investor I met in Europe in the forties. You are probably thinking, 'boring little fellow in a gray pinstriped suit and fedora, smoking a pipe and squinting through his wire-rimmed spectacles.' You are partially right, as you will see. But I do not think you will find him boring. On the contrary, he has a certain mystique, like those 'gnomes of Zurich' who are said to be sitting on the piles of the world's gold in the subterranean vaults of the Swiss banks, riding their rickety elevators upstairs once in a while to cast a cynical eye toward their computers and the world money markets, to ponder the flashing green numbers and all the people trying to get rich in a day on paper currency.

"He may be one of those gnomes. You will have to decide. But he knows more than any other man I have ever met about living well, about acquiring and maintaining wealth and using that wealth wisely.

"For now, trust me as you always have in the past, and follow the enclosed travel instructions. And when my dear friend takes you to that tiny restaurant hidden up the hill at the end of the cobblestone street, order the paella and think of me.

Love to both of you,

Your Grandfather

P.S. Carry the other sealed envelopes with you. Do not open them now. You will know when the time is right to reveal their contents."

Paul folded the letter and put it back in its envelope with the other sealed envelopes. What to make of it? "Now I understand why he quizzed us at such great length about our honeymoon plans," Paul said. "We must have made it easier for him when we said we were postponing a trip until we completed all our job interviews. He had his own trip in mind."

"I don't see how we can go," Julie said. "We have so much to do right now, the wedding gifts to pack and store, so many thank-yous to write, our apartments on campus to clean out...and then job interviews in just over a week.

"What could be so important that we need to jump on an airplane to a place we don't even want to go to meet a man we don't know?" She looked so perplexed, her head bent down as she used her butter knife to spread grape jelly on a triangle of whole wheat toast, that Paul wanted to leap across the breakfast table and wrap her in a comforting hug.

To tell the truth, he felt a bit perplexed himself. This was indeed a strange turn of events. What could be so important that his grandfather couldn't simply tell them? And what more could they learn? He and Julie had both worked hard in college, they had been conscientious students, taking grad-level courses in philosophy, economics, finance, the very subjects grandfather's "gnome" seemed to know about.

He felt a twinge of disappointment, even a touch of anger at his beloved grandfather. But he trusted him implicitly, too. How could he be angry at a man who had always, without exception, had Paul's best interests at heart? And he was surely wise in the ways of the world. His own life was proof of it. Most importantly, he had never let Paul down, had never disappointed him. Paul thought of his warm smile, his deep-set eyes that always seemed to convey love. His grandfather had always had that special ability of very wise people to see the world through a child's eyes, to explain things in a way that made sense to a child. Even the most complicated subjects like astronomy, mathematics, physics. He never ran out of patience or knowledge, it seemed. And he always knew a child's limits, how much a young mind could absorb.

His grandfather's greatest strength, Paul saw as he grew older, was his ability to get to the heart of things, to see the central truths. He had a way of sifting through a mountain of information to reveal the important fundamentals. In his years at the university Paul had seen academics who had lost sight of their relationship to the world, who had become overwhelmed by facts, minutiae, details that came to take on a life of their own. The newspaper pages were filled, too, with the sad stories of brilliant people on Wall Street, in law and other professions, who misused their gifts, who ended up with neither their dignity, the respect of their peers, nor their wealth.

"I think we should go," Paul said. "It doesn't make any more sense to me than it does to you, but I just have to believe that my grandfather knows what he's doing. He's never let me down before, and anyway, Switzerland should be beautiful in the spring."

"It's just such a shock," Julie said. "We were really counting on your grandfather to help us out, and we end up with two plane tickets and a letter and a bunch of mysterious little envelopes that we aren't supposed to open yet. I feel like Nancy Drew. The difference is she always knew what she was trying to figure out. We don't even know if we need to know whatever it is your grandfather thinks his friend knows that he knows we do need to know."

Paul laughed. "You're right," he said. "I don't think I can repeat what you just said; but you're absolutely right." He took a bite of his scrambled eggs, which were growing cold and distinctly unappealing. Somehow food didn't seem very important at this moment.

"Let's think of it as our first crazy married adventure, pack our suitcases, head for the airport, and see what happens," he said. "If we don't like what we see, well! turn around and come back. All we have to lose is a few days. Risk taking, intelligent risk taking, is something grandfather has always believed in, and we can consider this trip a small risk on his behalf. All we really stand to lose is a little time. He also believes in information gathering before making judgments, and in seeking the counsel of people you consider knowledgeable before making decisions. If we decide to come right back, he'll understand. He'll accept our judgment if he knows we investigated the situation first. But I know he'll be terribly disappointed if we don't go, if we don't evaluate his plan based on our own observations. I'm intrigued by this journey. I just know he wouldn't have suggested it if he didn't think it was worthwhile for us. What do you say?"

"You know your grandfather better than I," Julie said. "And I have nothing against an adventure in the Alps! After all, how many newlyweds get sent on a mysterious trip the day after their wedding? At least we'll have something to tell our grandchildren."

Chapter 4

Arriving in the Land of the Gnomes

The Geneva airport was barely visible as the 747 landed in the heavy mist. Paul and Julie had tried to sleep through the long night as they ·crossed the Atlantic, but their racing thoughts made it difficult to rest, to relax. Who was this man they were going to see? Would he really be there to meet them? Would they recognize him? And what could he possibly know that could be so important as to warrant a trip to Europe on a moment's notice?

In the terminal, their eyes scanned the crowds for the man who was to meet them, the man with the important secrets to their life success. They could see no one who looked like such a genius, who would know things they had never learned before and needed to know.

They had neither a name nor a phone number, just the envelope from Paul's grandfather. There was nothing to do but wait. They sat down, weary from the long flight and lack of sleep, feeling a little like orphans awaiting new parents. "Wouldn't it be funny if he didn't show up?" Julie asked. "Not very," Paul answered. "I'm the one who got you into this adventure, and I'll be pretty upset if it comes to nothing, if it begins and ends here in the middle of an airline terminal."

"Well, there's lots to do in Geneva," Julie said, leafing through the travel brochure she'd read at least five times through on their Swissair flight. "Now that we're here I wouldn1t want to miss the towering Jet d'Eau in Lake Geneva and the historic Town Hall, the beautiful Romanesque cathedra! of Saint Peter, the European headquarters of the United Nations and the famous monument to Reformation and ..."

"I think I married a travel agent," Paul interrupted, thanking his lucky stars for

Julie's good spirits. At that moment, a man, short in stature, wearing a three-piece pin striped suit and wire-rimmed spectacles, walked toward them, seemingly materializing out of thin air. He looked precisely as Paul's grandfather had described him in the letter. It had to be....

"Hello. Paul? Julie?" They stood up, nodded, smiled, their faces betraying their joint feelings of relief at his arrival. "Your grandfather described you perfectly. I'm sorry to be a few minutes late.

Your flight arrived a bit early, I think. I am Monsieur George St. Luc, your grandfather's friend for so many years.

He escorted them through customs and then through the huge terminal to the baggage pick-up area. His chauffeur-driven Mercedes sedan was waiting for them outside.

"I know you must be tired from your long flight," he said, "but there is much we must do in a short time, and you must be well rested. My driver will take us now to the small farmhouse in which my great-great grandfather was born. It is a few hours' journey from here through the springtime countryside."

As they drove along, Paul and Julie in the back seat holding hands, Monsieur St. Luc in the front seat next to his driver, they marveled at the beauty of the pale greenness everywhere. There were budding trees and spindly-legged young lambs and their mothers eating grass along the steep hillsides, which fell away from the endlessly curving roadway. So, relaxing was the journey that both Paul and Julie found themselves nodding off, nudging one another to stay awake as Monsieur St. Luc reminisced about his long friendship with Paul's grandfather. It was a friendship of young men now grown older, and he told of the strange turns of life that had brought them together, the things they had seen, the places they had been, of his grandfather's dreams for Paul and this moment. As the engine droned on, and mile after mile of pastoral landscape rolled by their windows, Paul and Julie found themselves drifting between slumber and consciousness. Monsieur St. Luc's soft accent further lulled them into sweet torpor, their immediate future entirely in his hands.

Chapter 5

The Lesson Begins

Very early the next morning they were awakened by the loud crowing of a rooster, who sounded as though he might be right under their window. Monsieur St. Luc had told them that would be their signal to rise and join him for breakfast.

The farmhouse was used now only for overnight visits and vacation stays, and it was kept exactly as it had been for more than two hundred years. Paul and Julie felt as though they were staying in a museum, which in fact they were, a monument to the hard work and perseverance of Monsieur St. Luc's ancestors who had lived on the land. The small house, built on stilts with space for the animals below, and all the furniture in it,

had been built from materials available nearby. There was a simple beauty in the starkness of the furnishings.

After a meal of fresh hard-crusted bread brought that morning from the village bakery, pale butter with the sweet aroma of mountain grasses in it, and strong tea made by heating water over the ancient fireplace in the kitchen, Monsieur St. Luc began his story.

"You are probably wondering," Monsieur St. Luc said 1 "why your grandfather, who loves you so dearly and wishes so much good fortune for you, has sent you at this golden moment in your life to this small country to sit in an old farmhouse with an old man you met only yesterday.

"The first answer is: For 'The Long View'. Age, if it teaches nothing else, nearly always teaches you that life is simpler than you thought. The beautiful simplicity of life is its grandest lesson, and the hardest to learn.

"The world's greatest thinkers, men and women who devoted their entire lives to understanding the human condition, have always derived ideas of the most sublime simplicity -the importance of love, the importance of work, the wisdom of treating others as you yourself would like to be treated.

"Truly understanding the simplicity of life's principles has never been more difficult than it is today. But it has never been easy.

"Whenever I have been in danger of forgetting it, I have always returned here to the farm of my ancestors. Without this little farm, and the lessons it continues to teach me, I wouldn't be the success I am today. You will see why by the end of your stay."

Chapter 6

The Farm

At that moment, there was a knock on the farmhouse door, and Monsieur St. Luc greeted a tall, muscular young man whom he introduced to Paul and Julie as Franz, the farm's caretaker. Franz, like Paul and Julie, was an economics student, studying at the University of Zurich in the fall and winter months, and working at the farm in the spring and summer to support his studies. He had the blond hair and fair complexion that one would have expected of a Swiss farmhand. "You remind me of the people in the story of Heidi and her grandfather that I loved so much as a child!" Julie said. "Being here is like having the story come to life." Franz smiled. "If you feel so now," he said, "you will feel even more so by the end of this day." With that, he pointed to the wall behind them where, on wooden pegs, were hanging rough-woven overalls and heavy jackets. "Put these on," he said, "and meet me in the stable."

After bidding Monsieur St. Luc good-bye, Paul and Julie left the warmth of the kitchen hearth, and headed out into the cold of a sunny spring morning. One could still see patches of un-melted snow here and there, and the green rolling hills before them seemed even more glorious than they remembered from their drive to the farm. "This is all pretty wild, isn't it?" Paul asked. "I never thought of us as the farmer and his wife, did you?"

"I haven't had time to get used to being anybody's wife yet," Julie laughed. They met a waiting Franz in the stable. "This farm is run exactly as it was several hundred years ago when Monsieur St. Luc's ancestors first began living here and supporting themselves from the land," he told them.

"They had no money when they began. The original few acres surrounding this farmhouse were given to them as a land grant in the middle of the 18th century, in much the same way that American settlers obtained their farms as homesteaders. They knew little more about farming than you do today at the start. They had only their hands, their bodies, their determination, and the need to produce enough food to feed their families. Today you will see how they did it."

With that, he handed Paul a pitchfork and pointed him to a wooden cart standing outside the stable. "Out there," he said, pointing to a haystack near the stable, "is breakfast for Annie and Agnes. Go and fill the cart and bring it back. In the meantime, Julie and I will set to the morning milking." The cart was heavier that Paul imagined, and it took concerted effort to pull it up the slight incline toward the haystack.

Back in the stable, Franz took to instructing Julie in the proper way to approach the milking of Annie and Agnes, how to soothe them, where to put the stool, the proper motion to use in expressing the warm milk from their full udders. The task, she discovered, was not an easy one, and it was only after repeated tries that she was able to achieve any success. Just at the moment that she was beginning to fill the wooden bucket, Annie shifted suddenly, and Julie, in her skittishness, kicked over the pail. It took her what felt like hours to finish the task, with continuing minute-by-minute instruction from the very patient Franz. Her hands ached, her back ached, and her shoes were damp by the time she completed her first farm chore, but her day had only begun.

The major task for the day, they discovered, was to begin clearing a new field forth spring planting of oats and corn. Much of the St. Luc land had been converted to non-agricultural enterprises in the last fifty years. What land remained was used as a living agricultural museum, so that schoolchildren could observe farming methods of the past.

"By the end of the day you'll be glad we don't have to depend on our labor for our food," Franz said. "I never truly understood how hard our ancestors worked until I began working on this farm."

With shovels, hoes, and rakes stacked in a small cart, they set out for the rock-strewn field, continuing their day's work. "I'm glad we're in such good condition," Paul told Julie. "Otherwise this might not be much fun." Julie agreed, and they followed Franz's lead in gathering the larger rocks and carrying them off to the side of the field where Franz planned to construct a long stone erosion barrier. The work was so demanding they barely talked to one another, conserving all their energy for the job at hand.

By the time the sun was overhead and Franz declared it to be time for lunch, they were both feeling more exhausted than from the heaviest of aerobic workouts. Under the shade of a tree, they sat down, happy for the break, and ate their lunch. It was the simplest of fare, more of the delicious hard-crusted bread and pale cheese they'd had at breakfast, along with apples and walnuts, and wonderfully cool mountain water which Franz brought in a heavy crock. "I'm exhausted," Julie said. "But we accomplished a lot this morning." It was true. They had gathered enough rocks that the beginning of a wall could be discerned which would eventually be the border for the entire field.

"It really does give you a sense of satisfaction," Paul said. "I never would have believed a pile of rocks could be so fulfilling." Franz laughed. "Seeing the results of your labor is one of the great joys of the farm," he said, "and it always reminds you of one of life's most basic lessons: How much you accomplish is directly related to how hard you're prepared to work.

"It was not an easy life to be a farmer a few hundred years ago," he continued. "These people lived, how do you say, on the edge?' in a way that we can hardly imagine. Their very lives depended on producing enough food to feed themselves, and they learned as they went along. It was only through years and years of back-breaking toil and hardship that they cleared the land, learned about the effects of changing weather conditions, seasonal patterns, soil conditions; insects, differing seed varieties and so on.

"In years of plenty they did well, sharing with their neighbors who had fallen on hard times, and in difficult years relying on those same neighbors for help. But as the next generation cleared more and more land, and learned more and more about agriculture, they eventually were able to grow excess food with which they could barter.

"Over time, succeeding generations gained knowledge of which crops were more reliable than others in the uncertain climate of the Alpine lowlands, and the value of rotating crops for increased yields. Because of unpredictable weather, they came to realize that it was better to grow a variety of crops, so that if one failed, you could rely on the one or two others that fared better under those conditions.

"With this increasing knowledge came increasing yields; and, eventually, there was money left at the end of each season, money to be saved for the future.

"Being good observers and keeping good records proved to be crucial to the St. Luc's success. They not only learned about the ways in which weather, soil condition and seed quality affect crop production: they also began to see patterns in crop prices and farm expenses as well, patterns which eventually would offer important lessons of their own. Slowly, slowly, over time, they prospered.

"It was in Monsieur St. Luc's great-grandparents' generation that the family began to take divergent routes. His great-grandfather Walter, the second son and a very progressive man for his era, decided to become one of the first students at the agricultural college in Basel. He returned with scientific and financial ideas that were to change his life and those of succeeding generations.

"Once he married, he decided not to live in the small family farmhouse as was the tradition for the newly married sons and their wives. Rather than pay rent to his parents like his older brother, he took all his savings and made a down payment on a small bungalow in the nearby village. There he and his family lived until his parents passed from this earth.

"It was then that Walter and his older brother, Peter, entered into an amiable financial arrangement, one which altered the direction of each side of the family forever.

"Each of the brothers inherited half of the farm, including the farmhouse. The older brother, Peter, no longer wished to live in the farmhouse, as he was averse to borrowing money to buy out his younger brother's half-interest. The younger brother, Walter, proposed that he move into the farmhouse and that Peter move into the bungalow. He would get a new mortgage on the farmhouse, pay off the bungalow mortgage, deliver it to his brother free and clear and make up any difference in the values of the two structures with a cash payment. The land was divided equally, with the older brother receiving the farmland nearest the bungalow while the younger brother received the land surrounding the farmhouse itself. Each brother was delighted with the fairness of the solution and they remained the best of friends even though the paths of their lived took them to very separate destinations.

"Peter's descendants, who followed his example, lived frugally on their small farms, making enough to live on but little more. A few of them are still here in this valley.

"Walter's descendants, Monsieur St. Luc among them, have by contrast lived lives of great enterprise, using the same simple concept that allowed Walter to mortgage his first small home, pay off the debt with his farm wages, and later, to mortgage the farm itself and pay off the debt with the income provided by the farm. Several of those descendants went on to pioneer some of Switzerland's most important industries. But I'm getting ahead of myself....

"By keeping his records from year to year, Walter proved to himself the major uncertainty in the farming business: crop prices. Depending on how many other farmers had grown the same crops and how many buyers there were, prices fluctuated greatly. Good years meant high yields, but lower prices. Bad years meant decreased yields, but higher prices. Neither situation was satisfactory. By rotating his crops, Walter was able to increase his yields, but not enough to overcome market fluctuations.

He needed to find a way to be assured that he would always make enough to survive and expand.

"About that time he learned of a certain prized grape which flourished in their valley, thanks to calciferous soils and plentiful sun. The value of this particular vine and its grape, he thought, was likely to increase from year to year with the increasing yield of the maturing vines and increasing demand for the grape.

"Gradually Walter and his family converted most of their land to the production of these grapes. Only a small portion of the land was used for annual crops, which they grew for their own consumption.

"At that time a small parcel of land adjacent to the farm property was offered for sale by the neighboring farmer. It was a new experience for Walter to venture beyond the family boundaries and he deliberated at great length about whether or not to buy the property. It entailed more borrowing than he had experienced in the past. Because he had maintained such perfect records over the years he was able to review his and the farm's financial growth in great detail and to substantiate what seemed to him to be self-evident truths.

"He reviewed the purchase of his original bungalow and how his mortgage payments were easily covered by his wages from the farm. After he added up all his mortgage payments and his original down payment and compared that sum to the very fair value for which he had traded it to his brother, it appeared that he had lived there for not much more than the cost of the mortgage and built a substantial asset at the same time. Could that be?

"Then he carefully reviewed the farm history. There had been no predictability in annual crop profits. But with the grape it was different. There, annual production was much more predictable and prices had increased most every year.

"He concluded that if he borrowed against the predictable income of the grape in the same fashion that he had borrowed against the farm income with the mortgage on the farmhouse, he could buy the land and pay back the loan from existing farm income as well as from the new vineyard income.

"If he slowly converted the new land to grape production while paying off the loan, he concluded, in time he would own a larger debt-free farm producing greater income than ever. He bought the land and was fortunate enough to be able to repay the loan on schedule."

With that, they gathered up their tools again, returned to the fields and spent the rest of the day moving rocks, turning over the soil with their wooden implements and removing the stubborn low-growing shrubs that stood in their way. They returned to the farmhouse just as the sun disappeared behind the mountain. Paul and Julie felt an acute exhaustion unlike anything they had ever known. "And we thought staying up all night studying for finals was tough," Paul said. "My muscles are telling me that this is more work than I've ever done."

"Me, too," Julie uttered, hardly able to think of another thing to say.

Back at the farmhouse, the splendid aromas coming from the kitchen inspired them to wash up and join Monsieur St. Luc in the living room to wait for dinner to be served. He poured them all small glasses of sherry and then began to review the day.

"Paul, you and Julie have completed your first day," he said. "You've touched the soil and have learned how hard the work can be. You'll be happy to know that because of your limited time, I'm not going to have you spend the three days in the field that I usually ask my young guests to spend."

Paul and Julie both laughed weakly. Neither of them could imagine another two days of such back-breaking labor.

"Let me explain to you the reason for the three days. It is to demonstrate in an

unforgettable way that there's more than hard work involved in success." He called out to the kitchen where Hans was helping his wife, Elsa, make final preparations for the dinner. "Hans, how many rocks did Paul and Julie carry today?"

"One hundred and eighty-six," Hans answered.

"It seemed like two thousand and four," Julie said.

"Most people carry between seventy-five and a hundred," Hans replied. "Between the two of you, you did the same."

"On the second day," Monsieur St. Luc continued, "we tell each person that he or she must carry sixty rocks just to earn their food and lodging. But every ten rocks they carry over that, they can exchange for a piece of a wheelbarrow. There are three parts to a wheelbarrow.

"We explain to them that a wheelbarrow can easily haul fifteen rocks over flat terrain and that by using a wheelbarrow on the third day, they will potentially reduce their time in the field by half. Their incentive is that they will have an afternoon off.

"Of course everyone carries enough extra rocks to be able to acquire a wheelbarrow on the second day."

"That's when the fun begins," Hans yelled from the kitchen.

"The next morning I ask everyone to follow me with their assembled wheelbarrows," Monsieur St. Luc related. "I lead them just beyond the field and down to the riverbed where there are ample rocks. I ask them to deliver those rocks to the same location they delivered rocks the day before. Then I leave.

"Hans and I wait for about half an hour or so and then we walk back to the river to join our rock movers. Of course, they're always frustrated because they have found that you can't use a wheelbarrow to push rocks up a hill. It's just too heavy a load.

"We don't address their frustration. We just ask them to follow us and to bring their wheelbarrows. Then we lead them back across the field to a rock-filled hillside and ask them to continue their work. And again, we leave.

"It's generally not an hour later that a happy worker is back in the farmhouse, having completed the task of moving the required number of rocks. With the wheelbarrow, going gently downhill, they are able to move twenty to twenty-five rocks at a time. As an earned reward, they are given the rest of the day off. When we meet for dinner, as we are now doing, we discuss the events of the day.

"What do you suppose the reaction of most people is?" Monsieur St. Luc asked Julie.

"1 would suspect that they usually tell you they felt tricked initially, because you never told them they would be pushing the wheelbarrow uphill," Julie replied.

"That's true," Monsieur St. Luc agreed. "But l point out to them that none of them asked, and if they had been good observers, they would have noticed on their first day that the field was not the only location where rocks were to be found."

"You're saying," Paul interjected, "that simple observation would have provided them with a lot of knowledge that might have led them- to ask questions that, in turn, might have better prepared them for their day's work and reduced their eventual frustration."

"Exactly," Monsieur St. Luc agreed. "And what else?"

"Well," Julie continued, "Everyone realizes from the outset that if they don't do a minimum amount of work, they aren't going to eat. It's a basic rule of survival."

"Right, and...?"

"And they also know that if they do more than the required work they will receive greater rewards: extra rocks can be exchanged for something else, in this case, a wheelbarrow."

"Do they learn anything about savings?" Monsieur St. Luc asked.

"Sure," said Paul. "In fact, it's a clear example of the results of saving and investing: greater productivity. You save the extra rocks to invest in a wheelbarrow which makes it possible to move more rocks in a shorter period of time, thereby receiving greater rewards in the future."

"Exactly, Paul. It's a trade-off of today's extra effort in exchange for tomorrow's rewards," said Monsieur St. Luc. "It illustrates the importance of hard work, discipline, perseverance.

"And there's one more thing they learn, too- the importance of moving beyond frustration and a sense of failure. When they're down there at the riverbank with that useless wheelbarrow, they realize they should have asked a few more questions first. But the wheelbarrow isn't really useless. They could have bartered it for something else or they could, as I had them do eventually, use it successfully in a different environment.

"It's one of the things your grandfather understood so well. Not all of his early experiments were successes. Many of them led nowhere. But the discovery of what didn't work was a valuable contributor to his future successes. The history of great science, great creativity, great entrepreneurship, is full of failure. That is generally the difference between entrepreneurs who succeed beyond their dreams and those who don't.

The ones who succeed use failure as a lesson, not as a sign of worthlessness or hopelessness. It's the single most basic step of all-- it's called 'perseverance'.

"Both hard work and failure can be steppingstones to success. Perseverance is key."

After dinner …a delicious meal of roast chicken and a French-inspired ratatouille of eggplant, tomato, potato, zucchini, peppers and onion prepared by Franz's wife, Elsa -Paul yearned to stay up and talk to Monsieur St. Luc. He wanted to learn more about his friendship with Paul's grandfather, why he and Julie were here and what it all meant. But he was too tired. Keeping his eyelids open as he gazed into the burning logs of the kitchen fireplace was simply beyond his ability at that moment. He noticed Julie's head nodding, too. They excused themselves, headed for their giant featherbed, and fell asleep in an instant.

Chapter 7

The Vineyards

The next morning, they were awakened by the now familiar crowing of the farm's enthusiastic rooster, and once again they joined Monsieur St. Luc for breakfast. Today, he said 1 they would be in for a new experience, since they would be turning their attention to the farm's vineyards. Paul said he was disappointed; he had dreamt of gathering rocks in his sleep and was sure he'd come up with a more efficient technique for building rows. "There is room for ingenuity in caring for grapes, too," Monsieur St. Luc laughed. "A day in the vineyards will perhaps provide you with another kind of vision of the future.

But first, more of the story. When my great-grandfather Walter had turned the vineyard management over to his sons, there came on the market one of the choicest pieces of land for many kilometers around, larger in dimension than the family's entire existing farm and vineyard. They had long admired its perfect slopes and gradual inclines, turned toward the southwest where it received maximum sun. They had often wondered why the man who owned it had not planted it with vines, but he was old and feeble and planned to move into the small village nearby where his daughter lived. This piece of land was terribly expensive by their standards; it cost much more than anything the family had ever bought, not just in terms of the money itself, but in terms of the money they would have to borrow compared to the farm yield they expected to receive. The payoff period would be a long, long time.

"Walter's brother, Peter, who was still alive, thought they were crazy for considering such a purchase, since the enormous cost of the land, and the borrowing it required, would mean a significant degree of risk on their part.

"Still, they coveted it, knowing its value to the family's future. And they had the experience of previous mortgages to show that borrowing money could be a wise decision. My grandfather Jacob and his wife, along with his brothers and their wives, made a difficult decision to borrow as much money as they could by mortgaging their homes, the family lands, everything they had. Everything!

"The payments of interest and principal, which they had never faced to such a degree before, seemed frighteningly prohibitive. But they calculated that if they bought nothing new and saved every franc they could from the production of the existing farm and the vineyards, with hard work and their knowledge of agriculture they could pay off the loan, even though it would take many years.

"The first year they planted only a few vines, and farmed the rest to ensure income from their rotating crops. They projected as closely as possible how much cash would be needed to pay the principal and interest on their loan from year to year, what crops would need to be grown, probable market prices and target yields.

"What they hadn't counted on was two successive years of near-drought which caused them to default on the loan in its second and third years, bringing the family to the brink of financial ruin. When the payments came due, they simply didn't have the money.

"They begged the seller for mercy financing, which he luckily agreed to. Still, their misfortune resulted in several years of severe belt-tightening as they struggled to regain their financial footing and repay the loan and penalties.

"The only reason they survived at all is that they got a couple of important breaks. Without a little luck, they could not have kept going. They were lucky that the seller agreed to extend the loan and they were lucky that demand increased for their grape, which was used in a wine that unexpectedly became more popular than they could have imagined.

If Sometimes all the good intentions in the world aren't enough; you need a little luck to come your way.

"Despite those bad years, though, they eventually recovered and found to their great happiness that they could eventually pay off the loan, primarily due to the vineyard, which became profitable more quickly than they dreamed possible.

"It was not that the grapes had grown faster than they expected. They had matured exactly as predicted; it was not possible to defy the laws of nature. The surprise was that, as time went by, both the demand for their particular grape and thus the grape's price kept increasing far beyond their expectations.

"The happy result was, despite their frightening short-term setback and severe penalties, they were able to pay off the loan.

"But it was not so easy as it sounds," Monsieur St. Luc concluded. "Today you will see what I mean."

"I don't know if I can survive another day of your education," Julie blurted. "I'm still aching from carrying all those rocks yesterday." She was quite serious, having dreamed of spending the day soaking in a nice hot tub, which the old farmhouse didn't have.

"You're sure this is how my grandfather meant for us to spend our honeymoon?" Paul asked. "It was my faith in him that led me to convince Julie to come here, but I have to admit that I'm beginning to have my doubts. Now I know why he left for a fly-fishing trip to Chile the morning after our wedding. He didn't want us to be able to call him!"

"He and I worked out your schedule with a great deal of care," Monsieur St. Luc said. "In fact, we have been working on this plan for more than twenty years, from the time you were a very small boy. It was an idea that came to your grandfather in a moment's inspiration, much as his idea for the electroplating process did. He remains confident to this day that it will prove of exceeding value to you, in much the same way that his invention has turned out to be of such exceeding value to him. He has always insisted that he has had only a few great ideas in his life, but that in a lifetime, a few great ideas are all a person needs. I believe he has proven himself correct."

At that moment, the smiling Franz appeared at the door and, like obedient if doubting children, Paul and Julie left the kitchen to put on their work clothes. The garments already had the look of authentic labors about them, encrusted as they were with the spring mud they had encountered yesterday and a tear or two from the jagged rocks.

The morning view from the farmhouse was sublimely beautiful, with the sun just tipping over the snowy peaks in the distance, transforming the dew-covered grass in their valley into a field of diamonds. They went below to the stables to wish Annie and Agnes a good morning, and then set off across the valley to the distant vineyards. Julie was relieved to find that Franz had already completed the morning milking. She was even more relieved to discover that no new vineyards were being contemplated, and that clearing land would not be on their day's agenda. But they were to discover that the maintenance of the established vineyard was no easy task either, when all the work had to be done by hand.

"Grapes are one of the oldest plants in the world," Franz told them. "Many Biblical stories mention the grape, and grapes appear often in the myths, fables and poetry of many peoples of the world. The original appeal of wine had nothing to do with its alcoholic content; it was simply much safer to drink than much of the water available to our ancestors. The Old World or European vinifera grapes, of which these are a hybrid, have been carried all around the world, and are the foundation of your country's grape culture, too. The planting of grapes on this farm added greatly to the wellbeing of Monsieur St. Luc's family, as you will see." He showed them how he had pruned the grapes earlier in the year, where the first spring leaves were now beginning to unfurl, and explained how to cultivate the soil around the grapes and why it is so important. With that, they took their wooden hoes and began working up and down the long rows of grapes, which were neatly trained to grow on wire trellises. The work was easy in the cool morning, but as the sun became hotter, they once again began to feel the strain of their labors.

"I can't imagine working this hard day after day, week after week, year after year." Paul said at lunch. They sat again with Franz, sharing their meal of bread, cheese and fresh fruit. "If you had mortgaged your whole future to the enterprise, it would be easier," Franz laughed. "The St. Lucs were happy to work this hard in order to guarantee that they would never be hungry, that each generation would find their lives a little easier and more secure.

As they worked through the afternoon, Paul and Julie found themselves caught up in Franz's attachment to the soil, in the sense of spirituality he seemed to derive from his work on the farm. But it was hard work, and they began to feel the heavy weariness they had felt the day before when long mountain shadows enveloped the valley and it was time to return to the farmhouse.

"You might think that life would have gone on unchanged forever in this valley and on this farm," Monsieur St. Luc said later as they ate their dinner. "But the development of railways throughout Europe brought my grandfather Jacob and his brothers into competition with farms at much greater distances. Once grain and other crops could be shipped from place to place, he had to compete with farmers whose land produced greater yields and who had more advanced farming machinery than he. This caused him a few years of disruption until he switched to other crops which, like the grapes, grew better here than anywhere else, and updated his farm equipment.

"Soon the farm became more prosperous than ever. All debt had been repaid and savings began to mount. It was at this time that the family decided to build a winery. Again, they had to borrow a great deal of money, but after the success of their earlier venture mortgaging nearly all they had to buy the vineyard land, they felt less fearful about moving into this new enterprise.

"They were willing to risk their savings and their time, but they were not willing to risk losing their farm or their home as they had almost done some years earlier. They determined never to bet the whole farm again, but to limit their borrowing and to carefully calculate the maximum loan payments they could carry, using the vineyard income.

"They knew now the reasons for trying to limit their risk, but they had also learned the great advantages that could come with leveraging their income. They concluded that they would only consider future ventures with manageable risk, that never again would they risk all. They had learned the laws of leverage.

"But enough. I know how hard you worked again today, and I myself feel the weariness of an old man with a full stomach and the warmth of the fire lulling him. Tomorrow will be an easier day, but we still have much to do. I will see you then."

"Monsieur St. Luc," Paul said, "I must ask you one thing before we go to bed. I have three envelopes from my grandfather, all of them sealed. Do you know about the envelopes?"

"Yes, I do, Paul," Monsieur St. Luc replied. "As I told you, your grandfather and I talked for many years about this very day. You and Julie were probably in kindergarten when we began talking about you being here, just as you two are now. But the time for the envelopes has not arrived. You can trust me that it will, and you will know the proper time. You have been patient enough so far to trust your grandfather in coming here, and good-spirited enough to dedicate yourself to the hard work that Franz has given you. With patience, you will find that the time for the envelopes will present itself."

Despite their fatigue, Paul and Julie stayed awake talking for some time, debating the merits of remaining to see what Monsieur St. Luc had in store for them. They knew they were under no obligation to stay. They had fulfilled their promise to Paul's grandfather by coming and Paul knew that his grandfather would accept their decision if they returned home. But should they?

"Working on the farm just as people did hundreds of years ago has been interesting," Julie said. "I'll never take food or wine for granted again. But why do we need to know about farming anyway? I don't want to grow wheat in Kansas! We should be interviewing right now with the big investment banking firms in New York. We haven't got any time to waste."

"I know," Paul agreed. "we put off our own honeymoon to start our careers, and wind up in a Swiss field. This is no honeymoon. I don't even have enough energy right now to act like a bridegroom."

"And I don't have enough energy to care," Julie said, cuddling up against him in the featherbed and feeling her eyelids growing heavier every moment. She fell quickly asleep to her husband's rhythmic snoring.

Chapter 8
The Winery

Springtime is among the most relaxed times at the winery, Paul and Julie discovered, very unlike the feverish fall activity surrounding the crushing of the grapes and the beginning of the fermentation process. Their third day began with Franz introducing them to Hans Schmidt, the longtime vintner and the man responsible for the chateau's fine reputation.

Paul and Julie were relieved to discover that from the beginning to the end, winemaking demands experience and skill acquired by much observation and practice under a learned eye, and that their unskilled assistance would not be required that day. Instead they had their first opportunity to act like tourists, visiting the great vats, the dark cool cellars with their mold-covered bottles quietly aging. They learned from Herr Schmidt about the long apprenticeship he had undergone to learn the wine-making art, and how, even at the age of sixty-two, he felt there was still much for him to learn. He showed them scrapbooks with pictures and ribbons from the many wine festivals in which he had participated. Herr Schmidt proudly explained the reasons that various vintages over the years had won awards when measured against the finest wines produced anywhere in Europe.

"Like most great enterprises in life, it is a long, slow process." he said. "But the rewards are many, and the work is always satisfying. I would not have chosen any other life." At lunchtime, he invited them to join him for his noon meal, and provided them with tastings of several bottles of his best wines, each one specially chosen to complement the flavors of the cheeses, smoked ham and fragrant pears on which they dined.

After lunch he suggested they go for a walk, and they accompanied him up a mountain path worn smooth by many footsteps over many summers. On either side spring wildflowers were in bloom. As they climbed higher, the view of the undulating farmlands, varying in color between the rich brown of newly turned soil and the pale green of the earliest spring crops was beautiful in a way they could not have imagined from below.

"I feel as though we've been here forever, and it's only been three days." Julie said, looking out over the valley and smelling the softly scented bouquet of violets she had gathered for herself along the path. "Time here seems to have a dimension of its own."

"In this place one is able to remember that time is a special gift," Herr Schmidt said. "It is the one gift we all share from birth on, but many forget the true value of the gift, its immensity. Here one remembers. And remembering, one learns patience, that hour upon hour, day upon day, year upon year, time, if used well, can bring you · your dreams."

Later that afternoon, when the vintner had returned to the winery, Paul and Julie hiked higher up the mountain, following the path suggested by their new friend. When they returned to the farmhouse, they felt joyful and peaceful both of them exhilarated yet calmed. They were at once beguiled by their surroundings and puzzled by their host.

"Monsieur St. Luc," Paul said at dinner, as they dipped their bread into the wonderful herb-flavored lamb ragout that the old gentleman had proudly prepared himself, "Julie and I are growing to love this place, as I am sure you knew we would, and you are treating us like royalty. But we still don't know why we are here. Your modesty has prevented you from telling us much about you, but we've heard about your reputation as an investor and philanthropist from Franz and Hans. We can see now why you and Grandfather are such good friends. It's obvious you're similar people. But we're still lost as to why you and Grandfather thought it so important for us to come here.

"So far," Paul continued, "we have learned that it is possible to be quite comfortable in very simple surroundings, that the plainest of foods, when mixed with fresh air and hard work, can taste superior to the finest cuisine, and that hard work and patience can pay off. And we know that the careful borrowing of money was important to the growth of the St. Lucs and their farm, that the long-term investment involved in grape culture and wine production proved to be wise. We know that because their expectations were not only modest but reasonable, the St. Lucs were able to exceed them.

"But these things we knew before, even if now they do have new meaning. Frankly, knowing your background, I'd be more interested in talking about international trade imbalances, protectionism, your own views on random walk theory and index funds, options and derivatives, the value of the dollar against European currencies, the potential for a gold crisis, and how Soviet democratization may affect European and American markets."

"Oh, I would love to talk to you about all those subjects." Monsieur St. Luc laughed. "As you may imagine, I have strong opinions about all of them, all or none of which may be right. And I am sure you do, too. In fact, let us begin right now, over our cognac and espresso."

And so, they talked into the evening, covering the whole range of world financial topics, solving global problems with the deft stroke of a well-placed phrase, enjoying themselves immensely. Having displayed their ability to understand and talk about complex financial subjects, Paul hoped that Monsieur St. Luc, who was clearly the brilliant financial strategist his reputation suggested he was, would understand that they needed no more of the simple lessons that could be gleaned from running the farm.

He intended to suggest to Monsieur St. Luc the next morning that they might learn some truly useful things if they could spend some time in Zurich. He liked the idea of getting closer to the places where the world's money was flowing in and out of the Swiss banking centers, perhaps even meeting some of the powerful people overseeing these international transactions.

But in the morning Monsieur St. Luc had other ideas.

"Today I will tell you the rest of the story," he told Paul and Julie as they finished their coffee at the breakfast table. "I believe you will then see how valuable this modest little farm has become to me over the years. You will see why sitting here at this roughhewn table, being warmed by the heat of forest logs, and looking out at the rolling valley below, I remember the important things. You will see why, sitting here, I can better appreciate the labors of my ancestors, the sweat and energy they expended felling trees to build this house, this very table, these chairs upon which we sit. And you will see why all of this has been more important to my success than any of my university degrees or my years of experience in banking and business management.

"Let us now seek out the morning sun, and begin the story with its warmth falling upon us." With that, they carried their chairs outside and found a place protected from the wind at the other end of the stable area where Anne and Agnes would come to be milked later in the day. The smell of the newly pitched hay seemed to mingle grass and sunshine. It was not a smell that suggested sophisticated international monetary genius, which was perhaps why Monsieur St. Luc chose the spot. Like the rest of the farm, it suggested only the fundamentals, the earth, grass, sky.

"Once my grandfather and his brothers had developed the farm, vineyard and winery operations into such profitable operations that they had excess cash to work with, they were presented with new challenges," Monsieur St. Luc began. "Perhaps another family presented with such profits might have been happy to stick the francs under the mattress and thank the Creator for their good fortune. And, in fact, my grandfather and his brothers thought about simply putting the money in the bank or buying government bonds.

"But they had learned important lessons that pointed them in other directions.

They had learned that dedication and time build financial comfort, that a proprietary product like their coveted grapes can build wealth, and that leverage created by borrowing to build ownership in real estate and business can either enhance or destroy one's fortunes.

"They knew that putting their own money to work for them, as well as making prudent use of lent money, were necessary to ensure that the family's fortunes would continue to rise. Ownership was the key. Keeping their hard-earned money in the bank or loaning it to others would only provide the opportunity for someone else.

"They began to search for other opportunities, remembering the lessons of the farm that they had already learned.

"Now that they were going out into the big world, however, Uncle Hermann suggested that they needed to know much more. And so, they began to subscribe to economic journals, to read the daily financial newspapers, and to spend time at the town library searching out economic and political texts. They studied the short-range and long-range economic trends of Switzerland and all of Europe. They studied the political makeup of the members of the Standerat, the Council of States, and the National Council, and tried to predict what policies they would likely put into effect in the years ahead. They looked at the economic and political situations in all the European countries and tried to predict the likelihood of war or peace. They looked at trade patterns around the world and where they seemed to be headed. They tried to discern how Switzerland would measure up against potential trade competitors. They soon discovered how little they knew about all of these areas. They decided to use some of their savings to hire experts from the great European investment houses and universities with reputations in investment and commerce to come here to farm and to sit with them, just as we are sitting here now I remember my grandfather Jacob telling me of these meetings, how impressed he and his brothers were with these scholars, with how much they knew about the world around them. My grandfather and his brothers, by comparison with these great men, felt very limited in their own learning.

"But here was the surprising conclusion they eventually came to: that even these learned men could not provide the answers they sought. Because of the multitude of unpredictable variables involved, there were no solid answers to the kinds of questions they were asking. Oh, everybody had hunches, good guesses, their own reasons for believing that one direction or another would be likely. But these great men themselves could rarely agree when it came to making predictions about the future. There were just too many unknowns, too many possibilities, too much room for unexpected developments. Nobody could predict economic trends. And there seemed to be no correlation between trends, let alone the success of individual businesses.

"And so, after all the learned scholars had gone back to Paris and Geneva and Heidelberg and Fribourg and Tubingen, my grandfather and his brothers were left alone again, sitting together as we are at this moment, looking out at the valley below them.

And they began to think anew about the farm, and about the questions they had asked when they selected their various crops, when they had decided to plant grapes, when they had decided to establish the winery.

"Eventually they realized that all those decisions, decisions that had been so vital to the success and happiness of the St. Luc family, had been based upon an entirely different set of questions, questions that had answers. Those questions were answerable and included such inquires as:

"What can we produce that other people here in Switzerland and elsewhere want to buy? What special skills or advantages do we have? What do we do better than anybody else? What are our limitations? What do we know that we don't know? And the most important questions of all: What have we observed?

"When they asked these questions, they began to see answers, answers they were sure of, answers that required no grand assumptions, answers that they could deduce by keeping their eyes open, by keeping good records, and by paying attention to what was going on around them."

Chapter 9

The Family Gathering

"Shortly thereafter," Monsieur St. Luc continued, "they had a legendary family meeting with all the brothers and all their wives and all their children old enough to have observed the farm and the vineyards and the winery over several years. They decided that, before making any investments, they should be clear on the principles that had brought them so much prosperity.

"They cleaned the floor of the big barn, and made a giant table of pine boards and sawhorses. They hung garlands of flowers to give the place a festive air, since they were planning an appropriately grand celebration when the meeting was over. They brought wooden chairs from all their houses, and used benches and barrels and makeshift chairs.

"They had gone to so much trouble to consult with the great academicians, who couldn't give them the answers they needed, that they decided they should certainly be willing to expend an equal amount of energy consulting among themselves. By now they were sure they had many answers between them, and that their own experience was very valuable, more valuable that they had realized.

"They held the meeting (we'd probably call it a seminar today) on a rainy summer day when it was too wet to work outside. Once the meeting started, they talked and talked without rest from dawn to dusk.

"They had a wonderful time, sharing family stories of the good times and the bad times, their triumphs, their mistakes. My father was only a small boy then, but he remembered being there with his mother and often talked about it. He would describe listening to everyone's voices rising and falling, his uncles puffing on their pipes and carefully tapping the ashes into big pottery butter crocks that had been brought in the barn for that purpose.

"There was so much to discuss that they met for a second day as well. All the brothers and their wives wanted to be sure that every good idea was heard, explored, examined and reexamined. Only then could they agree on the important principles they should take with them out into the world as they began to invest in enterprises far removed from the family farm.

"At the end of the second day, as my father would recount it, they had condensed all their thoughts into essential meaningful principles. Then came a great feast. There was much eating and dancing to the tunes of Aunt Bertha's pump organ, which they rolled out to the barn from her parlor, Uncle Frederick's fiddle and Uncle Wilhelm's tuba. My father remembered most fondly the music and the chocolate bon-bons and the ice cream. Perhaps the simplest pleasures are the most enduring."

Monsieur St. Luc looked off across the fields as though he were a boy again, listening to his father's stories. "My father and his cousins would have been too young to remember the thoughts that the family came up with," he continued after a long pause. "Perhaps that's why they hired the village sign painter to come and record the St. Luc family investment principles on the biggest wall of the barn to endure through the generations.

"Come. I'll show them to you now. They've faded a bit over the years, but they're as sound as ever. You might be surprised if you knew how many times I've come back to the farm over the years, just to sit on a milk stool in the barn and look up at them. Whenever I was overwhelmed with financial data, or investment choices, I could always gain a new perspective by coming here. '

It felt good to stretch after sitting all morning and they took the long route to the barn, stopping to say hello to Anne and Agnes in the dairy shed. Walking through the herb garden and the orchard, they admired the effect created by the falling apple blossoms, covering the ground with a lovely pink blanket of color.

Once inside the big barn, Paul and Julie were immediately drawn to the wall opposite the barn door, which Monsieur St. Luc had described. The St. Lucs' investment principles were painted in a beautiful calligraphic script that looked timeless and irrefutable on the rough barn wood walls.

Here's what was written there:
- There is no substitute for hard work.
- Learn from your failures; persevere.
- Observe and Learn
- Respect the laws of leverage.
- Patience and time are an investor's greatest allies.
- Remember the vine.

"That's it?" Julie asked. "Those are the lessons that explain the increasing success and happiness of generations of St. Lucs?"

"It's all there." Monsieur St. Luc said, smiling. "As I told you, I've returned many times over the years when I needed to settle my mind, to know if I was moving in the right direction, to gain the clarity which is so easily lost in the hurly-burly of the financial marketplace."

"But everybody knows those things," Julie countered, a note of disappointment in her voice. She had been hoping for something more, something dramatic, something hidden. For this she had crossed an ocean, postponed her job interviews, moved fieldstones and sweated in the sun cultivating somebody else's vineyard? "These are only what I would call the fundamentals of conservative investment. They're no secret."

"They may be no secret, but you'd be surprised how often they're forgotten," countered Monsieur St. Luc. "I can tell you stories of sophisticated, well-educated people who forgot them to their peril, who continue to forget them every day of their lives. They're not as easily understood as you might imagine."

"Remember the vine.' That's the puzzler. "Paul said, following his own train of thought. Julie was right, of course. But what about the last one on the list? "I agree with Julie that all the others are pretty obvious, and not very exciting, either. But I don't quite understand 'remember the vine'. What does that mean?"

"If you remember the vine, you will never forget any of the others." Monsieur St. Luc said. "That's why it's last on the list. It's really the most important one of all, because it ties the rest together.

"But I'm hungry and tired, and I'm sure you are, too. We're already late for a special lunch I have planned for you today. Let's go freshen up, and my driver will take us into Martigny to a favorite little restaurant of mine that I'm sure you'll love, too. A dear friend of my late wife and mine will join us there. I'm sure you'll enjoy meeting her." With that they left the barn and the St. Luc investment principles behind them, and headed up the hill back to the farmhouse.

At lunch, Paul and Julie, wearing their "town" clothes for the first time in days, felt as though they were truly on vacation. As they approached the restaurant, walking up a steep cobblestone path to reach it, Paul remembered Grandfather's note. "Do they serve paella here?" he asked Monsieur St. Luc. "Yes, Paul, how did you know?"

"The place looks just as Grandfather described it in his letter to us," Paul replied. "We must order the paella in his honor." Not only was the meal precisely the delight Monsieur St. Luc had promised, but his friend Mme. Nadolsky was a charming, intelligent lunch companion.

In her sixties, Mme. Nadolsky turned out to be a serious investor in the stock market, and they found themselves in the midst of an animated discussion of the potential attractiveness of several publicly traded companies.

"When I retire, I'm going to put all my money in the bank," Julie said. "I don't want to have to worry about the ups and downs of the market when I get to be your age. Where do you find such courage?"

"It's not a matter of courage," Monsieur St. Luc interrupted. "It's a matter of survival. Corporations and quality real estate are the safest places to put your money as long as you live." And then he added with conviction, "You'll know what I mean when you, too, have learned to 'remember the vine' and exchanged a knowing look with Mme. Nadolsky.

"But enough of that for now. You and Paul deserve some time to yourself. Mme. Nadolsky and I are going for a stroll in the park, and then I shall attend to some business matters here in town this afternoon. My driver will pick you up in front of the Hotel Des Alpes at 9 o'clock this evening to return you to the farm, where I will be waiting for you. In the meantime, you have a few hours to be alone, and to act like the honeymooners you are!"

With that he paid the bill, and made some suggestions of places they might want to visit around town. Leaving the restaurant, Paul and Julie sat down on a bench under a hanging basket of gaily blooming geraniums and petunias to discuss their afternoon plans, as Monsieur St. Luc and Mme. Nadolsky, hand in hand, headed down the street in the direction of the lakeside park.

"Remember the vine," he called back to them as they walked away. "Remember the vine!"

"What do you suppose that means?" Paul asked. "I haven't the foggiest notion."

Julie laughed. "But I want to know. If we can be as happy and as comfortable at their age as they appear to be, I'll be satisfied. They must be doing something right."

Chapter 10

Remember the Vine

The next day Paul and Julie met Monsieur St. Luc once again for breakfast in the old farmhouse kitchen. They told him of their day's adventure in town, the places they visited, the souvenirs they bought, the fun they had listening to the brass band playing by the town fountain at dusk. "And now and then we whispered sweetly into one another's ears, 'Remember the vine,'" Paul laughed. "You've really piqued our curiosity."

"Yes, you've got our attention," Julie said. "We want to know about the vine."

"The vine, ah, yes, the vine. Remember the vine," Monsieur St. Luc mused. It has been the secret of my success, of all my brothers and their families, and you grandfather, too.

"It was because of the vine that my family became involved in the banking industry, a decision that over the years has proven to be a very lucrative one indeed.

"You will remember that at the end of the first family conclave everyone had agreed on several principles, including one having to do with the power of leveraging derived from borrowing against one's income. They had seen their fortunes grow when they borrowed money astutely to purchase good farmland. The income from farming the land increased over the years while the cost of their loan did not. The interest rate and the monthly payments were fixed. It was the same with the vineyard and the winery. Income increased; loan costs remained stationary.

"Going back over their records for many years they noticed something else. Not only their income from the farm, but their income from the vineyard and the winery was increasing. The price of nearly everything went up from year to year. They were observing the phenomenon we now call 'inflation'.

"And they discovered something else of equal significance; money they had in the bank over time earned a rate of interest that was always about the same as the then current or prevailing rate of price increases. This discovery that inflation rates more or less matched interest rates was important because it made clear to the St. Lucs in a dramatic way that putting your money in the bank was no way to make it grow.

The rate of interest you received would be about equal to the rate at which prices were increasing, so the net increase in your purchasing power would be very small.

"They now understood that loaning money to others, whether to the bank in an interest-bearing savings account or certificate of deposit or to the government or a business in the form of a bond, was a move worthy of caution. One could make more money by owning than by lending.

"The income they earned from what they owned…the farm, the vineyard, the Winery…increased at a rate faster than inflation. This was partly because many of their costs, such as mortgage costs, were fixed, and did not go up with inflation. Other factors contributing to their growing income were increasing productivity (they could use the same machinery to farm more acreage, for instance), increasing sales volume, (as the grapes and wine were made available to larger and larger numbers of people, and increasing market share as the reputation of their grapes and wines grew.

"So they knew they should use their extra money to buy ownership in a business enterprise, either their own or somebody else's. But what business? They listened to the ideas offered by others. On the surface, they all sounded good, some even too good to be true. Slowly they eliminated alternatives. They eliminated all the ideas they couldn't understand. They eliminated the get-rich-quick ideas, remembering that patience would lead to slowly earned fortunes that endure. Besides, they wanted to remain wealthy, not get richer by accepting higher risks.

"Always they tried to remember the vine. What did it mean? It meant to look for businesses that would endure because they had a unique character, a quality all their own that couldn't be easily duplicated --like the St. Lucs' special grape that grew only in that small region of the Alps. It meant to look for businesses that would grow slowly, soundly, surely. It meant to be patient, to believe in the future. It meant to be a careful borrower. And more....

"During this time my grandfather, by chance, met the president of the principal bank of Zurich, a man he had known in college. Their conversation, as it often does with entrepreneurs, turned to their businesses; and grandfather asked his friend what probably seemed to be a naive question; How do banks make money? In grandfather's experience, he had made money by borrowing money, not lending it, and he couldn't quite understand how banks could make money by lending money.

"Oh, we don't loan our own money," the banker told him. "We loan other people's money.

"Banks are founded with a small amount of money," he said, "but most of the money they work with is money borrowed from their depositors, those people who put their money in the bank in order to receive interest on their savings. The bank then re loans those deposits. The difference between what the bank pays depositors and what they receive on loans, about a 2-3 percent spread before expenses, is left for the owners of the bank."

"Swiss banks were in a particularly strong position, the banker told him, because of special qualities that no other banks in the world enjoyed, making them especially appealing to depositors around the world. Switzerland's long history of neutrality and stability and their privacy laws made their banks particularly attractive.

"As a result they didn't have to pay high rates of interest to their depositors because they had so much else to offer. Since they didn't have to pay high rates of interest, they could charge lower rates on loans and as a result, they could pick from among the soundest of applications.

"To grandfather it sounded like another version of the vine, a stable, growing industry with a product special enough to protect it from competition. 'It's the vine all over again," he mused, "just another version of the vine."

"If we invest in the banking industry as part-owners, we will find much opportunity for growth, an opportunity lost to bank depositors," grandfather said. His banker friend, who tended to wear an inscrutable, taciturn look most of the time, apparently gave him an uncharacteristic sly smile.

"For the next fifty years, the St. Luc family invested much of their surplus funds in the banking industry, a position the family still holds today. In those years, they decided that the watch industry also looked like a lucrative place to invest. One of my uncles knew a German watchmaker of great experience and reputation who had managed a large business. The family decided to hire him to run our factory, which was then built. All the signs seemed right: it was easy to find many employees who were precise and skilled with their hands, few natural resources were required, transportation cost were low. Indeed, the enterprise looked as though it would succeed for a time, but soon there appeared factors which at first had not been obvious.

The competitive nature of the industry changed. Cheaper mass-produced watches using new technology ate into the fine watch market. Competition from the many other Swiss watch factories with generations of experience, plus the weakening of the overall market, left us unprotected. We recognized the negative change, but were trapped. There were no buyers for our business.

"We closed the factory, wiser than before. We had learned the hard way, as so many entrepreneurs do, that not all enterprises succeed, and that the unknown future always holds lessons of its own. We not only lost the money we'd invested, but were responsible, of course, for the money we'd borrowed as well. But at least we did limit our losses --we hadn't 'bet the farm', as you Americans say. It reinforced our position that manageable risk is acceptable. We got out of the business as soon as it was clear there was no hope of a profitable future.

"We converted the watch factory to a museum. Today the museum is filled with rare watch-making tools from the 19th century and with samples of the finest hand-crafted clocks and watches ever made in Europe, Asia and the Mideast. The museum is renowned for its displays and visitors from all over the world come to see them.

"For us, though, it is mostly a reminder that even great ideas can fail and that failure adds to our continuing learning process."

Chapter 11

*The Vine and Some 20th Century Inventions; Taxes,
Depreciation, Cash Flow*

"**A**ll the successful St. Luc family investments proved
the wisdom of the vine's lessons," Monsieur St. Luc
summarized.

"The vine taught us:

- the value of patience, of being content with steady growth
- that ownership of productive enterprises offers the only real
  protection against inflation
- the competitive advantage of proprietary products or services
  with special attributes.

"Like the St. Luc grape, which is grown in very few areas, our other
enterprises also had a proprietary element protecting them against
competition. In the case of the banks, it was the proprietary nature of
the entire Swiss banking industry.

"When looking for ways to invest we always kept the vineyard
principles in mind. But my generation had to learn a whole new
lesson, and it came about because of the advent of personal income
taxes and business taxes, something no previous generations of St.
Lucs had ever had to deal with.

"Let's go into the chart room adjacent to the barn, and I'll show you
why taxes made it so much more difficult to evaluate the worth of
enterprises, including our own farm and vineyard."

They left the kitchen and walked across the sunny farmyard. The
chart room, by comparison, was dark and dingy. An odor of ancient
moldy paper hung about it. "This room may not seem very appealing
on such a beautiful day, but my grandfather would come in here
and sit for hours on a Saturday afternoon," Monsieur St. Luc said. "It
was his place to think, to retreat from the week's hard work and the
family bustle of the farmhouse.

"He loved all the paper in here, and what it represented to him. He was fascinated by the numbers, the trends, the things you could learn simply by keeping records over time and looking for patterns. The price of corn, the price of apples, the cost of a plow, a horse, the interest rate on a loan. My own fascination with the world of numbers and finance I am sure began here. The first pictures I ever drew were on old ledger paper that Grandpa gave me right at the little table there."

The walls of the chart room were covered with yellowing sheets of paper tacked up with small nails, the ink faded with the passing of years. Piles of ledger books were stacked on all available shelves and tabletops. In one corner sat a small computer, a new acquisition demanded by Franz to keep his own records.

"In this little room you can see how keeping records became more and more important to the success of the farm." Monsieur St. Luc said. "In the earliest days, their charts on the wall, simple as they were, sufficed. For the next generations, ledger books became a necessity. And today, it does indeed help to have a computer to track the operations of a farm even as simple as this one is now.

"Taxes, as we 20th century taxpayers know, are quite straightforward when it comes to their effect on profits. They're a minus, a debit, a cost of doing business, plain and simple. After you've paid them, the money is gone forever.

"But the introduction of modern taxation brought with it another new wrinkle that wasn't so straightforward: the concept of depreciation. It's taken investors of my generation most of their lives to begin to truly understand how the depreciation allowance affects the value of business."

"That makes me feel better," Julie said. "In every business course I've ever taken, my eyes always glazed over when the professor started talking about depreciation."

"Well, you're not alone," Monsieur St. Luc said. "The concept of depreciation is simple enough, but its implications sometimes are not. Grandfather would have had to study his charts a long time to figure it out.

"As you know from your business classes, "depreciation" is just a way of estimating the life span of business property such as this barn, the grapevines, the plow, and so on. The theory is that because things wear out, the tax-paying business owner should be allowed to set aside a certain amount of tax-free income to build his or her versions of the new barn or new plow to replace the ones that have worn out or become obsolete.

"All the assets of a business, except the land upon which it rests, are considered to have a fixed life. At the end of this arbitrarily defined fixed life, they are considered to have no further value, which is to say that they have depreciated over time to a point of no worth.

"Thus depreciation directly affects how a corporation reports the worth of its assets. And depreciation, you will soon see, also affects how a company reports its profits.

"These, needless to say, are matters of great importance to an investor like me. But do these numbers tell you the true story? Do they really tell you what a company is worth?

"And the answer is ... it all depends.

"Some assets, like certain machinery or vehicles, for instance, do wear out eventually and become worthless. High-tech equipment like computers can lose value very quickly as it is replaced by better and cheaper equipment.

"But many other assets, like the grapevines, can increase in value year after year after year, even though their valuation for tax purposes goes down. It's one of the few times we can tell the government a 'legal lie'.

"As my grandfather discovered earlier, there can be many reasons for an increase in the value of certain assets over time. In the case of grapevines, for instance, there is the maturity factor. Older grapevines, instead of wearing out, produce even greater harvests of grapes because of their stronger woody stalks and larger root systems. Another has to do with reputation. As the special qualities of our grapes became more widely appreciated over the years, they were desired by increasing numbers of vintners. And perhaps most

important of all -- inflation, the slow, continuing increase in price
of nearly everything -- made the land, the buildings, the grape vines
and the grapes themselves increasingly valuable over time.

"Look at these figures here and you'll see how depreciation also
affects the reporting of profits." Monsieur St. Luc pulled down from
a shelf one of the newer looking ledger books. "For the year shown
here, a single grape vine produced profits of $5. At that time the
tax collector defined the life of the grapevine as ten years, and the
original cost of the vine as $20. Thus, each year, for tax purposes, the
vine lost $2 in value, and at the end of ten years had no value at all.

"Because the vine, for tax purposes, was losing value, the tax
collector did not require that we pay taxes on the entire $5 profit.
He subtracted $2 to account for the vine's supposed loss of value
that year, and taxed us only on the remaining $3. So, we freed $2 of
income from taxation. We paid a corporate tax of 35 percent on the
remaining $3, which was roughly $1. So, we were left with about $2
in net profits plus the $2 of income which was not taxed because of
depreciation. The $2 saved thus accounted for a healthy one-half of
all tax-free income and after-tax profits earned that year.

"More importantly, the income from the vine was actually
increasing, and therefore the value of vine itself was increasing,
because of the factors I mentioned earlier: maturity, reputation,
inflation.

"When, as a young man, I began to keep the farm records myself,
I didn't really concern myself with the implication of this increasing
income, except that I saw it as useful money that we could invest in
more land and other enterprises. How it related to the ultimate value
of our farm and vineyard escaped me. We had no intention of selling
the farm or the vineyard, so their market value was immaterial
to me. l knew that the depreciation allowance was a tax savings
designed to offset the vineyard's supposed loss of value over time,
and I knew, even as my grandfather had observed, that inflation
continued to slowly push prices upward and that most everything in
the vineyard was actually increasing in value.

"But from my grandfather's vantage point, there were only two numbers that mattered. He had always measured his expenses against his income, and felt satisfied if he was coming out ahead and had enough money to live on comfortably.

"As I looked at all these numbers and then included the depreciation figures year after year, I knew they meant something new in terms of evaluating business worth. I just couldn't figure out what they meant. All I knew was that we were saving taxes and gaining cash as an offset to what was supposed to be loss in value of the vines, but that the vines were actually becoming more valuable. I knew this had to be to our advantage. But it took me, and the rest of the world, too, some time to figure out how to evaluate such an advantage."

"Well, I feel much better about deprecation now," Julie said. "I've understood every word you said, Monsieur St. Luc, and I'm especially happy to discover that most of the world had been as confused about the subject as I have been. In fact, now I'm actually intrigued by what you say. If I hear you correctly, what you're saying is we can increase our chances of making wise investments by paying attention to the combined effect of taxes, depreciation and inflation."

"Yes, indeed, that is what I am saying," Monsieur St. Luc said.

"So, tell us more," Paul said. "Exactly how do we do this? We're certainly not going to have any money to invest for a while, but we will someday. You've definitely convinced us that investing in productive enterprises with long-term growth potential is the way to go, but how?"

"For the moment, let me just say this," Monsieur St. Luc said. "The world is a lot more complicated today that it was a hundred years ago, but grandfather's focus on income as a measure of business success is still right on target.

"Always look to a company's income statement first when you're trying to evaluate company worth. First you want to know how much money they are bringing in (revenues) and what their expenses are. The difference between the two is income or net earnings.

"But then you must factor in that complication of the modern age that grandfather didn't have to contend with…depreciation. If you add back the depreciation to the net earnings, you will have a much more accurate sense of the actual money the company has to work with…its cash flow. This is one of the most important of all numbers in evaluating a company's worth.

"A company's balance sheet includes a listing of all current assets, such as land, buildings, machinery and so on, minus liabilities such as debt, is usually a much less accurate reflection of a company's worth. The value of the farmland on the books, for instance, bears no relationship to its actual value today, since we bought it for so much less so long ago. And the stated value of our grapevines bears no relation to their actual value either, because of depreciation, inflation and their maturity.

"Sometimes you can detect hidden untapped value in certain assets, such as land, that could be put to more productive use. When we switched from crops to grapes, for instance, the income-producing ability of our land increased considerably, and thus the business net worth.

"But, in general, the income statement is the place to look for the most accurate and useable data for measuring current and future company worth.

"The proprietary nature of a company will also affect its value, though. The numbers for two companies might be identical, but their future value might be quite different, depending on how proprietary is the nature of their businesses. Are they doing something that few others are doing or do they have many, many competitors offering very similar services or products? There is judgment involved in deciding just how proprietary a business is, but it will certainly affect its future value."

Monsieur St. Luc looked at his wristwatch. "We've been in this musty old chart room long enough. It's time for some fresh air and a trip to town."

Chapter 12
The Chalet at Glacier Pointe

The next morning at breakfast Monsieur St. Luc announced with a smile that the "lesson of the day" involved swimming, hiking, steam baths, massages, great food, dancing and an overnight stay in the luxurious suite of a resort hotel with a view of snow-covered peaks.

"My favorite kind of schooling," Julie sighed happily.

"And not a word about depreciation or cash flow?" Paul asked hopefully.

"Well, I won't promise that," Monsieur St. Luc laughed. "But I will try to work it in before lunch."

Soon his chauffeur appeared at the farmhouse door, and they were off down the winding road that led them away from the farm and the vineyard. A light spring rain was falling, but it didn't dampen Monsieur St. Luc's enthusiasm for the day's adventure, nor Paul's and Julie's either. They hadn't been disappointed yet by Monsieur St. Luc's surprises.

"Today we are going to the Chalet at Glacier Pointe," he announced triumphantly.

"It has been the financial achievement of my lifetime, and proof that the investment principles my grandfather, my father and I devised, each according to our own time and our own experiences, were indeed sound."

"This is a place that belongs to you?" Paul asked.

"To me and other members of my family and investors who saw the same potential as I," Monsieur St. Luc said. "Including your own grandfather."

"I guess I do remember him mentioning something about a mountain resort when I was younger," Paul said, "but it didn't mean much to me at the time."

"It will mean something to you now," Monsieur St. Luc said. "The Chalet at Glacier Pointe is a wonderful example of investment principles working the way one would wish them to work.

"In the early forties, my father had turned much of the family's financial management over to me. It was a time when we had substantial cash flow as a result of the profitability of the vineyards, the winery and our part-ownership in several highly successful banks. I began looking for a way to invest that money in a new enterprise. Through the war years and the years of European recovery after the war, I made no decision.

"Eventually, though, the advent of commercial jet travel and the perennial desire of people to enjoy themselves with their families gave me an idea. There were already a number of successful ski resorts throughout Switzerland, all of which had achieved their major growth after the invention of the T-bar lift some years earlier. The T-bar, unlike the funiculars and cable cars of the past, reduced the long uphill ride to minutes. But most of these resorts operated only in the winter. It occurred to me that a year-round resort, one that incorporated not only skiing in the winter but summer activities as well could become a very profitable enterprise.

"I spent the better part of the summer of 1953 in my automobile, covering the areas within close proximity to the major international airports, looking for a site that would be appropriate for such a resort. I had with me a man who had designed ski slopes in Europe and the U.S., a building contractor, and an engineer. If you could have observed us that summer as we drove through the most scenic parts of the country, hiking up and down steep hills, studying the views from above and below, you would have thought we were on a marvelous holiday. We stayed overnight in little inns where the housemaids aired the goose down covers over the balcony railings in the morning and where the patrons in the breakfast room would greet you with a hearty salutation in French or German or English or

Italian. We hardly looked as though we were doing serious business. But we were. We must have examined two dozen sites before we discovered the one that was to become Glacier Pointe.

"Less than an hour from the Geneva Airport, my ski slope designer pronounced one location as pure perfection for both beginning and advanced skiers. In addition, it had a beautiful lake perfect for summer recreation, for sailing and swimming. We discovered that the owner of the acreage had never envisioned any higher use for it than as a summer pasture for his goats, and was happy to sell at a reasonable price.

"When you see the hotel and the ski slopes, the beach and the boathouse, you might think they have always been there. We made great efforts to preserve the natural beauty of the site, to use an architectural style and scale that would cause the buildings to blend into their natural surroundings. But such environmental aesthetics, we discovered, are neither cheap nor easy to create. What started out as a two-year multi-million-dollar project became an even more expensive four-year project before we were ready to open our doors. It took a great deal of faith on the part of my family and other investors like your grandfather. We had no choice but to increase our debt in order to build the resort that l had envisioned. We had no way of knowing for certain that the project would be a success. But as you know, risk and reward always travel together. It's impossible to hope to make money on the basis of anticipated growth without accepting some degree of risk.

"But I felt strongly that we would succeed, and we did. It was several years before we made any profit. But from the start, Glacier Pointe did what I hoped it would do…attracted families from all over Europe and later North America who wanted to vacation together in a place where there was something for everyone to do, winter or summer. It was no surprise that we didn't make money for some years. If you remember the vine, after all, you remember patience. Once built, though, we did begin to turn a profit sooner than anticipated."

"What was it that made Glacier Pointe different?" Paul asked. "I know how much importance you place on the proprietary element, the uniqueness of a product or service that makes it stand out in the marketplace."

"Ah, you begin to know me well," Monsieur St. Luc laughed.

"What I did that had not been done before, the proprietary element in the venture, was to target market appeal toward children. There were many other ski resorts and wonderful spas in Europe, but there were no such places where children could also have a great time while their parents were relaxing.

"From the start we had a children's ski school in the winter, and a children's water sports school, as well as nature and crafts instruction, in the summer. In the public areas, we used some of the appealing characters from the famous European fairy tales in large murals and hired college students to dress up as some of these characters to welcome arriving visitors and to escort them around the grounds. We designed a special children's dining room where children could eat their lunches unattended by their parents, and watch a movie or cartoons afterward.

"We used the fairy tale themes in all our advertising, and even began to sell shirts, hats, and other souvenirs with the Glacier Pointe logo on them, a little boy and girl much like Hansel and Gretel, on skis ...

"Much of this may not sound so original today, but in the fifties, it was very unusual. And it worked. Today we have men and women who were here as children bringing their own families to ski in the winter and hike and swim in the summer. Always, of course, we have had to keep up with the times. Children do not stay the same from generation to generation, and neither do their parents. Now we have added jogging and exercise facilities, a cooking school, vegetarian items to our menu, computers to both our ski school and our summer school, an outer space motif to many of our murals. We have a huge selection of favorite family films that can be viewed in your room, a dinner club as part of the adult evening entertainment. A July music festival, featuring outstanding jazz musicians from around the world, is now in its eighth year and has helped to spread the Glacier Pointe name far and wide, bringing guests to our door who would not otherwise have discovered us.

"We are developing computer software that creates simulated ski runs at every skill level, and allows users to practice various techniques and hone their skills before they actually go out to the slopes. There appears to be a worldwide market for this software, and we are now in the process of licensing manufacturing and distribution rights.

"Thirty-plus years after the opening of Glacier Pointe, our profits are greater than ever, and show no signs of slowing down. Our revenues have doubled in the last five years alone!

"But no matter how new and innovative some of our programs and marketing techniques may seem, it is the old family principles, remembering the vine, that have inspired and informed all of our decisions. As with the grapevines, time, maturity, reputation and the relentless influence of slow inflation have all combined to make our initial investment worth many times the original value of the real estate, buildings, ski runs, our schools and programs.

An attractive wooden sign, with the words "Glacier Pointe Resort" carved into it, came into view, and they began ascending a wide curving drive lined with tamaracks and spruce. Charming baskets of begonias and ivy hung from the lampposts. "I'll bet what comes next is the contribution of depreciation and cash flow to the continuing good fortune of all the Glacier Pointe investors," Julie offered. I know we won't get out of this car before we've heard about depreciation and cash flow one more time. "In fact, I think I know the story well enough to tell it myself."

"Well, you're right, of course," Monsieur St. Luc said. "Depreciation and cash flow are such critical factors in the operation of any successful enterprise today they simply cannot be underestimated or overlooked. I do recall promising Paul I'd work them in before lunch, though, and it's already 11:30. So, tell us what you know."

"The Glacier Pointe buildings, ski runs, copyrighted training curricula, clothing, souvenirs, software programs - they're all being depreciated over time according to various schedules," Julie began. "And most of the items, while worth less on paper for tax purposes, are actually increasing in value. The result is that you have extra cash to work with, thanks to the tax-free income created by your depreciation allowances, while at the same time nearly all the Glacier Pointe assets are increasing in value. It's a win/win situation; your income goes up while the value of your property and other assets also goes up."

"But what about our high maintenance costs?" Monsieur St. Luc asked. "It isn't cheap to maintain a huge resort and ski runs and summer boating equipment in excellent condition, you know. Labor and equipment costs have gone up tremendously over time with inflation, too."

"Yes, but I'll bet you've been able to increase your room rates and ski run prices at a rate exceeding that of inflation," Julie countered with confidence. "There's the reputation and resultant demand factor, just as with the grapes, and besides, many families today have more discretionary income than they have ever had, perhaps because they are having fewer children and many more women are achieving professional success. Yes, I'd be willing to bet that you have easily offset your costs due to inflation with greater price increases, and that your ability to do so will continue into the future because of the proprietary nature of your business. No one else has quite the same package to offer."

"Well, we can eat lunch now," Monsieur St. Luc laughed. "You've learned your lessons well, and there is nothing left for me to say, except 'bon appetit'!"

Lunch was a beautifully arranged plate of smoked fish, fresh greens, an entree of roast chicken delicately flavored with rosemary, and raspberry mousse for dessert. Then Monsieur St. Luc introduced Paul and Julie to a friendly green frog (later to become a prince, he said) who showed them to their suite. It was a spacious and elegantly appointed room with a large balcony overlooking a flowing stream. The frog offered to show them about the grounds and tell them about the various activities from which they could choose during their stay. They opted for a game of tennis, a short hike along one of the marked nature trails, and then a soak in the hot mineral bathes followed by massages.

"I feel as relaxed as it is possible to feel," Julie mused at the end of the afternoon as she stood on their balcony enjoying the scent of pines and the long view toward the snowcapped peaks, backed by the sinking sun in the distance. "This

feels like the honeymoon we weren't going to have for a while. I can see why Glacier Pointe has been such a success."

The next day Paul and Julie asked Monsieur St. Luc if their mysterious schedule could possibly permit another day at Glacier Pointe.

"Only for study purposes, you understand," Paul kidded him. "We haven't had time to visit the ski slopes yet, and gaining a full understanding of your operation here certainly requires that we do so, don't you agree?"

"Like a good investor, I am always trying to anticipate," Monsieur St. Luc laughed. "And I did indeed anticipate that your 'research' might require another day here at Glacier Pointe. Especially since the ski conditions in this part of Switzerland are their best in the spring, and the weather on

the upper slopes is perfect today. We, in fact, have nothing on the schedule until tomorrow, and the day is yours."

"A good investor always takes advantage of opportunity when it presents itself too," Julie said.

"And we see an opportunity here that shouldn't be ignored --a day on the slopes!"

"You will find yourself observing something about cash flow in spite of yourselves," Monsieur St. Luc predicted. "Much of the popularity of Glacier Pointe is due to the continual upgrading of our equipment and slopes. I have never hesitated to put a significant portion of available cash back into the resort, and the expenditures have proven wise. Our reputation for safety and skiing pleasure is unsurpassed."

"We'll be happy to offer our expert opinions at dinner," Paul said. "See you then!"

Chapter 13

Observe and Learn

The next afternoon following their return from Glacier Pointe, Paul and Julie found themselves heading towards town for a visit with Mme. Nadolsky.

"Mme. Nadolsky has always been a wise manager of her money," Monsieur St. Luc said. "All the years she was employed as headmistress of a girl's school, she managed her personal finances prudently. But now that she is facing retirement, all of her good sense and confidence are in peril. She asked if I would come and talk to her today, and I of course agreed. I told her that I would bring you along - that we could all learn together." She seemed the most confident of women the day we met her." Julie said. "I can't believe she would feel so lost.

"We all come to such points in our lives now and then," Monsieur St. Luc said.

"That's what good friends are for, don't you think?"

Mme. Nadolsky's apartment was unlike anything Paul or Julie had ever seen before. To them "apartment" recalled the tiny spaces they had occupied as college students. But this was different, a grand old residence with a marble-floored foyer, a spacious parlor with soaring arched windows that reached from the floor to the tall ceiling, wagged in rose-printed drapery fabric that fell to the floor in great folds. The huge room was filled with somewhat worn but lovely antique furniture, the sofas covered in a soft peach velvet. Everywhere were the mementos of a happy, busy life: children's drawings, family pictures, travel souvenirs.

"Welcome to my home." Mme. Nadolsky invited them to sit on the sofas positioned on either side of the small fireplace, which Julie imagined crackling warmly on a snowy winter day. Mme. Nadolsky herself was dressed for the occasion. She wore a soft green crepe suit with a silvery-gray ruffled blouse reflecting the color of her hair. Julie was glad that she and Paul had dressed for the occasion, too. Going to tea, Monsieur St. Luc had suggested by the tone of his voice, was an important event, and she was relieved that they had read him correctly.

Seeing the elegance of Mme. Nadolsky's living quarters, Julie was certain that she must have inherited money from somebody. While the room didn't suggest great wealth, it did suggest more comfort than Julie imagined a headmistress could attain. She was intrigued to hear what this pleasant woman, who seemed to live such a comfortable life, would have to say on the subject of money. What, Julie wondered, would be her version of "remembering the vine?"

After tea was poured and a tray of tiny apple pastries and petit fours had been brought from the kitchen, Mme. Nadolsky sat down in a chair between the two sofas where Paul and Julie and Monsieur St. Luc were seated. "I'm so glad you came today," she said. "I am so pleased to be celebrating my retirement after so many years. There are many things I want to do with my newly available time. But I'm feeling some fear and confusion. For the first time in my adult life, I won't have that paycheck to look forward to every week. Monsieur St. Luc has been helping me prepare for this moment for years, but still I feel great apprehension.

"I have saved money, and multiplied those savings through careful investing with Monsieur St. Luc's help and encouragement, but now I feel the time has come to put all that money in the bank and be as cautious as I can, and he is telling me otherwise."

"Oh, I agree with you." Julie said with great feeling. "When I retire I want to know that my money is safe!"

"Ah, yes, safety," Monsieur St. Luc mused, biting into a little cake with gusto. "I think it's time for us to go for a little stroll."

"But you just got here," Mme. Nadolsky protested.

"We'll drink our tea and then we'll go for a short walk down Villette Strasse," Monsieur St. Luc said. "It's only a few blocks from here, and we'll all be back in no more time than it takes to heat the kettle for our next pot of tea."

It was clear that Monsieur St. Luc was not going be deterred from his plan, and so after drinking their tea, they all headed out the door and down the street toward Villette Strasse.

"Simple observation," Monsieur St. Luc declared as they rounded a corner, "can tell you a great deal. I think that's why my grandfather and his brothers put it on their list of principles of investing."

"That house right there. Who lives in it?" Monsieur St. Luc asked. They were now on a street of imposing residences, surely among the finest in town.

"That's where the Rubenstein family lives." Mme. Nadolsky answered. "I had their daughter Sarah as a student. They own a leather goods factory. The father is an engineer and the mother is a commercial designer. Their purses, wallets and briefcases are sold in the finest department stores.

"And that house there?" Monsieur St. Luc asked, pointing to an equally imposing home across the street. "Oh, that's where Dr. Huss lives. He is a physician known throughout Europe for his orthopedic surgery."

"And how about that one there?" Monsieur St. Luc asked, as they made their way down the street of beautiful houses and beautiful lawns. "Oh, that's where Michael Saviski lives. He owns the Golden Rooster restaurant where you had lunch, as well as restaurants in Luzerne and Berne. They are all renowned for their excellent cuisine and service. He went to one of the best French cooking schools as a youth."

"Aha," Monsieur St. Luc said, as though he had discovered the crown jewels.

"And what about that one?" He pointed to an attractive mansard-roofed mansion enclosed by a beautiful brick wall. "The Berthold family lives there," Mme. Nadolsky said. "Monsieur Berthold runs a metal products factory which was founded by his grandfather after the First World War. He himself is a graduate of the Harvard

Business School. It seems to me that they produce parts used in the manufacture of automobiles."

"Good, good," Monsieur St. Luc said, as though he were quite pleased with himself. "And that house up the hill?"

"Oh, there's a nice story behind that one as you well know, Monsieur St. Luc. A barber, Wilfred Little, and his wife and their six children live there. He won 10 million francs in the Irish Sweepstakes four years ago."

"Now we shall walk back by way of Amden Strasse," Monsieur St. Luc said.

"Observe, observe!" Paul and Julie and Mme. Nadolsky all looked at one another, and raised their eyebrows in unison. "We are, we are," Paul laughed. "We're not exactly sure what we're seeing, but we're observing, we're observing." They walked several blocks back toward the center of town until they came to a street of fine apartment houses. "Do you know anyone living in any of these buildings along here?" Monsieur St. Luc asked Mme. Nadolsky. "Of course!" she replied, as though he might be losing his mind. "A headmistress eventually knows everybody in town, especially if they've been here as many years as I."

"So?"

"Well, in this building there is a dentist, a bank manager, a high-ranking customs official, a newspaper editor, and an owner of a hardware store. I believe I have seen a man I know to be a jewelry designer going in and out of this building as well. But I don't know everybody, you know."

"What about the building next door?"

"The head librarian of a major pharmaceutical firm, a professor of history, an engineer and a woman who deals in antiquarian books."

"Aha! Exactly as I would have predicted," Monsieur St. Luc said. "Do you see what I am getting at?"

"That people with more money can live in bigger residences than people with less money." Julie said.

"Or you could say that most people enjoy a standard of living equal to their earning ability. But there is more to it than that," 1 Monsieur St. Luc said, standing on the street corner as they waited for the traffic light to change. "Who has the most money?"

"Let's see," Paul said. "In those great houses up the hill there was the leather factory owner and a restaurant owner and the physician in private practice."

"And the owner of a metal products factory," Julie added.

"Don't forget the barber!" said Mme. Nadolsky.

"So?" asked Monsieur St. Luc.

"So the people with lots of money all own their own businesses," said Paul.

"For the most part, you will find that people who can afford mansions like those on Villette Strasse own their own businesses," Monsieur St. Luc said. "And those who live in moderate comfort like the residents of Amden Street usually have the next best thing from an income standpoint, successful careers. "Except for the barber," said Mme. Nadolsky. "He is employed by one of the hotel salons."

"He represents the good luck factor," Julie said. "The only way to be really rich without owning your own business is to win the lottery, I guess."

"Or to inherit the money," Monsieur St. Luc said. "Your chances of becoming very wealthy through luck or inheritance are both extremely limited, however. But not everyone aspires to great wealth, and you don't need great wealth to be 'very comfortable.'"

"Precisely," said Mme. Nadolsky. "I am proof of it myself. Let's go back to my apartment, which is very comfortable, and enjoy our tea. There we can talk about how to be a little bit wealthy, if not very."

Back at Mme. Nadolsky's, Paul had a question for Monsieur St. Luc. "If we took the same walk down a street of upper middle class people in America, what do you think the generalizations would be?"

"Oh, it could be anywhere in the world." Monsieur St. Luc replied. "The general observations won't change. You will find that:

1. nearly all the homeowners have college educations,
2. most have worked many years in the same profession, building experience and income,
3. thanks to inflation, a majority will have made most of their earlier accumulation of assets through the house they own,
4. most of them will accumulate 90 percent of their invested assets in the last 10 to 15 years of their work life. Why? Their expenses are greatly reduced after 50 since the children are grown and have graduated from college, their house mortgage is paid off, and their incomes are reaching their peaks.

"And as they grow older, they usually have one more thing in common," Monsieur St. Luc added.

"When they reach retirement age, they want to safely maintain their standard of living."

"This is exactly the story of my life," Mme. Nadolsky said. "I have a college education. I stayed with the same profession for many years. I bought this apartment with a small down payment, thus leveraging my modest income, and have watched it increase in value over time. I accumulated most of my investments in the past fifteen years, by investing my extra money in publicly traded companies. Thanks to Monsieur St. Luc, l knew that was the most sensible way to make inflation work for me.

"But now what? I need a new plan now that I am retired. My retirement goals are like most everyone else's, including, I suppose, the people on Villette Strasse and Amden Strasse: I want to maintain my same standard of living, including my residence or even increase it if possible, and keep my assets so that my heirs will have something to inherit."

"Retirement does represent a whole new challenge," Monsieur St. Luc said. "It's when inflation begins to work against you."

"A scary thought," said Mme. Nadolsky, biting down nervously on her apple pastry.

"Welt the good news is that you only need about 70 percent of your income to preserve your lifestyle after retirement."

"It's enough to make you want to run out and start a factory so that you'll end up with so much money it won't matter," Paul said.

"Not a bad idea." Monsieur St. Luc said. "But not one that will work for everyone, as we said earlier."

"And certainly a little late for me," said Mme. Nadolsky.

"Retirement, like the mass-produced automobile, penicillin and nuclear power, is a 20th century invention," Monsieur St. Luc went on. "Our forefathers didn't face the challenges of retirement that Mme. Nadolsky and I face. In an agricultural economy, there was no such thing as retirement. You were born, raised and died on the same farm. Food and shelter were pretty much guaranteed. You never stopped working, and you never had to contend with that other 20th century invention, the income tax.

"But today retirement means a dramatic alteration in one's financial picture. Earned income stops while inflation and taxes go marching right along. What everyone would love to do is {/freeze" their income, as well as the prices of goods and services the day they retire, and live happily ever after. But in reality, they should prepare for continuing inflation and taxes over their next quarter-century of life.

"People, as they reach retirement age, tend to overlook where they have been and where they are going. But, Mme. Nadolsky, 20 or 25 years ago, you were earning about one-third to one-half of what you earned this past year.

"Part of this gain in income came from your career advancement, and part came from inflation. You never had to be overly concerned with the consequences of inflation on your spending because your increased income more than offset it. But what would have happened to your living standard if you hadn't received a raise for the past 20-25 years?"

"Oh, I would be in terrible shape," Mme. Nadolsky said, furrowing her brow at the thought of it. "l would have had to spend all my money and I would have had to find smaller and smaller apartments to live in. I wouldn't have this fine apartment, and I would be without any of my investments."

"Therein lies the retirement dilemma," Monsieur St. Luc said. "Your earned income not only stops increasing, it stops altogether. But the price of everything you buy continues its relentless march upward. The key to retirement is to replace an ever increasing wage income with an ever-increasing investment income that will last for the rest of your life. The unhappy alternative is to reduce your standard of living year by year.

"Oh, I don't want to do that," Mme. Nadolsky cried.

"Well, then you must continue to take advantage of the enterprise of others," Monsieur St. Luc said. "It's never too late to invest in other people's businesses."

"But the only way she can do that is by owning common stocks, and stocks go up and down," Julie said. "What will happen to Mme. Nadolsky if she keeps her money in stocks, as she has in the past, and stocks go down?"

"Stocks will go down," Monsieur St. Luc said. "They have always gone both upward and downward in the short term. But the behavior of her investments over the short term can be of no consequence. She is looking at a life expectancy and, thus, investment time frame of 20-25 years."

"But what should Mme. Nadolsky do?" Julie asked with great consternation.

"She needs safety, and now that she's retired her earned income is ending. She can't risk investing in publicly traded companies as she has in the past, can she?"

"Can she not?" Monsieur St. Luc asked as he began pacing up and down the length of the living room between the sofas upon which they were sitting. "Can she not?"

"Real safety means preserving your purchasing power, and there is no investment in the world that will protect your purchasing power and protect you against price volatility at the same time. You must accept the volatility in order to protect your purchasing power.

"But before you agree with me, let's consider the possible economic trends upward and downward. There are really three: deflation, inflation and hyperinflation.

"Let's consider deflation first. Deflation is a decline in the prices of goods and services, which means that currency becomes more valuable. With severe deflation, prices of businesses decline as income of all kinds falls. Every dollar or franc increases in purchasing power. In the 20th century, deflation of any consequence has occurred only once, in the 30's. So, one must ask, what are the chances of such deflation occurring in the next 25 years?"

"Nobody knows," Paul said. "That's the problem."

"But we must plan for the future based on some intelligent probability," Monsieur St. Luc said. "To spend all of your life indoors to avoid the chance of a tree limb one day falling on your head would be to miss a great deal of fine weather and pleasure out of doors. Unless you had reason to believe that it was very likely that the tree limb was going to fall on you, why would you choose such a course of action? If you look at the historical record, we have had deflation in only three of the last hundred years."

"OK," Paul said. "Let's say there's a 10% chance of any prolonged deflation occurring sometime in the next 25 years. I suppose it's no greater than that. We ought to allow the possibility that it might occur, however."

"Fair enough," Monsieur St. Luc said. "Now let's consider the probability of hyperinflation, such as has occurred in countries like Argentina, Brazil and even Japan in the early seventies. Prices go up very rapidly, while currency value declines dramatically. What are the chances of hyperinflation occurring in a politically and economically stable country like Switzerland or the U.S.?"

"Not very likely." Paul said. "Probably no greater than deflation. Maybe 10 percent?"

"Fair enough again. That leaves us with everything in-between deflation and hyperinflation --the most likely scenario probably being moderate inflation such as we have observed for most of this century. If the probability of deflation is 10 percent, and the probability of hyperinflation is 10 percent, then the probability of something in the middle is 80 percent. Right?"

"Right." Paul said.

"Even though the greatest probability is that we will continue to have moderate inflation for the next 25 years, let's look for a minute at the consequences of our worst- case scenarios.

"If we have our money in the bank, and deflation occurs, we win. Our money is worth more as prices go down. Our purchasing power increases. So, there is a 10 percent chance, or so we're guessing as intelligently as we can, that putting our money in the bank or in some other fixed-income investment is the best decision we could make."

"If we have our money invested in corporations, and serious deflation occurs, the value of our investment will most likely decline.

"But serious deflation, such as we had in the early thirties, doesn't last. In time, it is followed by a return to slow inflation. Eventually our financial worth will improve.

"But it may take a long time. We must accept the fact that there is a chance that business ownership could be the worst course of action in the short term.

"If we have our money in the bank and hyperinflation occurs, we really lose. This is the worst of all possible worlds. Our money is worth less and our purchasing power declines dramatically. We can never catch up. Again, remember, we estimate this to be only a 10 percent probability.

"If we have our money invested in corporations, and hyperinflation occurs, the value of our investment increases at least by the amount of inflation, since costs, selling prices and profits all go up at least the rate of inflation. This is exactly what has happened in countries like Brazil.

The business owner has won while everyone else has lost.

"The point is, though, that neither of these worst-case scenarios is very likely. The greater probability, based on what we have seen in this century, is that moderate inflation will continue.

"You will have to admit that a great many people find market volatility scary, though." Paul said. They'd rather be in CDs and bonds and sleep well at night."

"How can they sleep well when they are assuming the biggest risks of all?" Monsieur St. Luc said.

"I still don't see what you're saying," Julie said. "Money in the bank is guaranteed and money invested in business is never guaranteed. How can you say that the bank is the bigger risk --especially after a person has retired?"

"Because inflation is the biggest guarantee of all," Monsieur St. Luc said. "As we have just agreed, the probability of slow to rapid inflation in the next 25 years is about 90 percent! And you can never beat inflation with a fixed investment.

"All we have to go by are the facts," Monsieur St. Luc said. "Observation is our best and only tool. And based on observation, these are the facts of retirement in the late 20th century:

1. A person who lives to be 65 years of age is likely to live another 20 to 25 years on the average. To plan your finances for fewer years than that is to risk being penniless before you die.

2. Inflation is a permanent factor in modern life. In the world, today it ranges from something like 3 percent to 2500 percent annually, depending upon which nation you look at. In politically and economically stable countries like Switzerland and the U.S., it stays down at the low end of the range. But we must assume, based on observation, that it will remain a factor throughout our lives.

3. Taxes are a permanent factor in modern life. There is no reason to believe that taxes will be abolished, and every reason to assume that all of us here, throughout our lifetimes, will likely pay taxes on our income that will consume 20 to 40 percent of our earnings annually.

"Because of inflation and taxes, the person who retires has two choices:

1. Live on a fixed income (pension, social security) and reduce the standard of living each year,

2. Increase income each year to keep up with inflation.

"Let's keep it simple," Monsieur St. Luc said. "Let's assume that a person who is retiring has $1 million to invest and needs a pre-tax income of $60,000 per year. This person has no other source of income. How can he or she best ensure that the $1,000,000 will provide security?"

"Today a fixed-income investment offers a 6 percent return," Julie said. "If your person puts the money in these securities, then he or she will have the money needed."

"But will they?" Monsieur St. Luc asked. "The reason the return will be 6 percent is because inflation averages near three percent. Remember that the rate of inflation usually approximates current interest rates within a few percentage points. If they need $600,000 the first year of retirement, they are going to need three percent more the second year in order to preserve the standard of living. That means income needed the second year is $61,800. And one should keep in mind that in Switzerland 35% of this income will go to taxes.

"If the fixed income investment provides $60,000, they will have to take an additional $1,800 out of capital.

"So, going into the third year of retirement, they now have only $998,200 in capital, and an income need of about $61,800.

"As you can see, it's a terrible trap. Income needs increase every year and the capital base has to decrease to make up the difference.

"A $1 million capital base providing a six per cent return won't last 25 years if your pre-tax income need at the beginning of retirement is $600,000 per year, you wish to preserve your standard of living, and the inflation rate is three percent. By pursuing this form of investment, a person virtually guarantees that their standard of living will decline dramatically and that they will have no money left when they die. Their estate will precede them. This chart demonstrates the point."

Fixed Income Investments
Withdrawing 6% Per Year/No Taxes

	Asset Value	+	Annual Return of 6%	–	No Taxes	–	Beginning income need of $60,000 increasing by 3% per year	=	Asset Value at End of Year
Year 1	$1,000,000		$60,000		$0		$(60,000)		$1,000,000
Year 2	$1,000,000		$60,000		$0		$(61,800)		$998,200
Year 3	$998,200		$59,892		$0		$(63,654)		$994,438
Year 4	$994,438		$59,666		$0		$(65,564)		$988,541
Year 5	$988,541		$59,312		$0		$(67,531)		$980,323
Year 6	$980,323		$58,819		$0		$(69,556)		$969,585
Year 7	$969,585		$58,175		$0		$(71,643)		$956,117
Year 8	$956,117		$57,367		$0		$(73,792)		$939,692
Year 9	$939,692		$56,382		$0		$(76,006)		$920,067
Year 10	$920,067		$55,204		$0		$(78,286)		$896,985
Year 11	$896,985		$53,819		$0		$(80,635)		$870,169
Year 12	$870,169		$52,210		$0		$(83,054)		$839,325
Year 13	$839,325		$50,360		$0		$(85,546)		$804,139
Year 14	$804,139		$48,248		$0		$(88,112)		$764,275
Year 15	$764,275		$45,856		$0		$(90,755)		$719,377
Year 16	$719,377		$43,163		$0		$(93,478)		$669,061
Year 17	$669,061		$40,144		$0		$(96,282)		$612,922
Year 18	$612,922		$36,775		$0		$(99,171)		$550,527
Year 19	$550,527		$33,032		$0		$(102,146)		$481,413
Year 20	$481,413		$28,885		$0		$(105,210)		$405,087
Year 21	$405,087		$24,305		$0		$(108,367)		$321,026
Year 22	$321,026		$19,262		$0		$(111,618)		$228,669
Year 23	$228,669		$13,720		$0		$(114,966)		$127,423
Year 24	$127,423		$7,645		$0		$(118,415)		$16,654
Year 25	$16,654		$999		$0		$(121,968)		$(104,315)

The picture gets worse if you need to live on the $60,000 and have to draw down from principal enough to pay taxes, as this chart presents.

Fixed Income Investments
Withdrawing 6% Per Year/Taxes

	Asset Value	+	Annual Return of 6%	–	Taxes of 35%	–	Beginning income need of $60,000 increasing by 3% per year	=	Asset Value at End of Year
Year 1	$1,000,000		$60,000		$(21,000.00)		$(60,000)		$979,000
Year 2	$979,000		$58,740		$(20,559.00)		$(61,800)		$955,381
Year 3	$955,381		$57,323		$(20,063.00)		$(63,654)		$928,987
Year 4	$928,987		$55,739		$(19,508.72)		$(65,564)		$899,654
Year 5	$899,654		$53,979		$(18,892.74)		$(67,531)		$867,210
Year 6	$867,210		$52,033		$(18,211.41)		$(69,556)		$831,474
Year 7	$831,474		$49,888		$(17,460.96)		$(71,643)		$792,259
Year 8	$792,259		$47,536		$(16,637.43)		$(73,792)		$749,365
Year 9	$749,365		$44,962		$(15,736.66)		$(76,006)		$702,583
Year 10	$702,583		$42,155		$(14,754.24)		$(78,286)		$651,698
Year 11	$651,698		$39,102		$(13,685.65)		$(80,635)		$596,479
Year 12	$596,479		$35,789		$(12,526.05)		$(83,054)		$536,687
Year 13	$536,687		$32,201		$(11,270.44)		$(85,546)		$472,072
Year 14	$472,072		$28,324		$(9,913.52)		$(88,112)		$402,371
Year 15	$402,371		$24,142		$(8,449.79)		$(90,755)		$327,310
Year 16	$327,310		$19,639		$(6,873.50)		$(93,478)		$246,596
Year 17	$246,596		$14,796		$(5,178.51)		$(96,282)		$159,930
Year 18	$159,930		$9,596		$(3,358.53)		$(99,171)		$66,997
Year 19	$66,997		$4,020		$(1,406.94)		$(102,146)		$(32,536)
Year 20	$(32,536)		-$1,952		$683.26		$(105,210)		$(139,015)
Year 21	$(139,015)		-$8,341		$2,919.31		$(108,367)		$(252,803)
Year 22	$(252,803)		-$15,168		$5,308.87		$(111,618)		$(374,281)
Year 23	$(374,281)		-$22,457		$7,859.90		$(114,966)		$(503,844)
Year 24	$(503,844)		-$30,231		$10,580.72		$(118,415)		$(641,909)
Year 25	$(641,909)		-$38,515		$13,480.08		$(121,968)		$(788,911)

"In either case, what you can see is that at a six percent return, your capital will precede you! You will run out of money before your life is over, the culprit being taxes and inflation.

"That's terrible!" Julie moaned.

"Better to know than not to know, don't you think?' Monsieur St. Luc asked. "Once you know the facts, you can make realistic plans."

"Unfortunately/ those people who need to make their assets grow after retirement are usually the ones who are least likely to do so. They often lack both the knowledge and temperament needed to make such decisions, which is one of the reasons they enter retirement with so few resources."

"Well that isn't the way I want it to turn out, "Mme. Nadolsky said firmly."

"I don't want to be a burden to anyone. In fact, I want to die with money left over. I want my attorney to be able to call a meeting and tell my nieces and nephews of their good fortune."

"Well, then, you must structure your assets so that your investment returns will take-up where your earned income has left off. While inflation is working against you on the income side it must work for you on the investment side. It will help to remember this little retirement formula:

To maintain your standard of living your investments must return your needed income plus inflation plus taxes.

Chapter 14
The American Gnome

The next morning at breakfast, Julie generously spread her toast with the exquisite wild strawberry jam Franz's wife had made earlier that week. "I'll never be able to taste strawberry jam this good anywhere else," she said, and then made a confession to Monsieur St. Luc. "I really didn't want to come on this trip," she said. "But now I don't want it to end. I've learned so much, and have had such a good time doing it."

"Learning should always be pleasurable, or it will never be remembered," Monsieur St. Luc said. "That was part of the genius behind Paul's grandfather's idea for this trip. But do not lose heart. It isn't over yet."

"You know what I haven't figured out yet?" Paul interjected, "is what all this has to do with us and the lives we plan to lead. Neither Julie nor I have entrepreneurial aspirations, although you've surely convinced us that that's the way to become very comfortable.

"And we'll never forget the lessons of the vine: the value of patience and time in building assets, the slow, positive effects of inflation on the value of one's assets and on the profits of a productive business in an enviable market position.

"We'll surely purchase our first home as soon as we can, to begin taking advantage of reasonable leverage and the benefits of inflation."

"But what about depreciation and cash flow? They matter enormously to a business owner, but how do they matter to us?" Paul asked.

Monsieur St. Luc posed his own question in reply. "Have I convinced you that investment in productive enterprise is one of the surest routes to well-being and a life that ensures opportunity of whatever kind you may desire?"

"Indeed you have," Paul replied.

"Well, then, my remaining task is to show you how that can be done without becoming an entrepreneur, and that is exactly why you shall meet a friend and trusted financial adviser of mine today. I call him my American gnome, but his real name is Michael Barnes. We are to meet him in an hour at Mme. Nadolsky's apartment. She has agreed to host the meeting because what he has to say is important to her future as well."

"I'll ask no further questions until then," Paul said. "Except one." He gave Monsieur St. Luc a mischievous look. "I've been wanting to ask it from the first day we arrived. Are you one of those fabled gnomes of Zurich?"

"Are Hansel and Gretel real?" Monsieur St. Luc asked in reply. "Do green frogs turn into princes and ride off on great steeds to rescue beautiful damsels in distress, delivering them to their castles on the spires of cloud-draped mountains?"

"Perhaps they are; perhaps they do," Paul said, with great seriousness, in contrast to Monsieur St. Luc's questions. He was thinking of how much the children at Glacier Pointe seemed to believe in the characters there, how much pleasure they derived from such fantasy. "They are real enough to influence your cash flow at Glacier Pointe, and that is about as real as anything needs to be."

"Well put, well put," Monsieur St. Luc said. "About as real as a gnome needs to be, too."

When they arrived at Mme. Nadolsky's, she greeted them at the door with great enthusiasm, and ushered them into the living room where a handsome dark-haired man in his early 50s with the studious look of a scholar and the pin-stripes of a Boston banker awaited them.

Michael Barnes, it turned out, was neither scholar nor banker. He was an investment analyst and portfolio manager, who, he told Paul, had been his grandfather's financial adviser for many years.

"It was through your grandfather that I first met Monsieur St. Luc," Mr. Barnes began, "and it is because of your grandfather that I am here today.

"Many years ago when your grandfather's invention was first beginning to bring him large royalties he asked Frederick Smythe, a senior partner in my firm, now retired, to manage his investments. Your grandfather apparently knew little about financial management and investing and wanted to devote his attention and energies to his work. He and Fred had gone to school together, and he trusted his intelligence and judgment. They developed a relationship of great mutual respect, which endures to this day."

"Your grandfather certainly did believe in his advice," Monsieur St. Luc said.

"When I began looking beyond my homeland to invest my own money, he insisted that I must join him to meet Fred Smythe. It was quite a meeting."

"I remember it well myself," Mr. Barnes said. "I was a junior partner in the firm at the time, and Fred suggested that I sit in on the meeting, that I might learn something. Did I ever!

"Fred began by explaining that our firm concentrated its investments in the common stocks of business enterprises because, over time, their rate of return had been so superior to any other form of income-producing assets.

"Monsieur St. Luc said that it was certainly consistent with his family's experience, that they had made all their money in their own business enterprises."

"It was about our only point of agreement however," Monsieur St. Luc recalled.

"We had quite a tussle, a battle royal. Two armies amassed on either side of the table, one yelling 'earnings!', the other screaming 'cash flow!' I knew little about investing in publicly traded companies at the time. All my experience had been in my own businesses, in the farm, the vineyard, the winery, the banking industry, the watch factory, the Glacier Pointe resort. I knew a great deal about running a business at that point, but nothing about the world of stock investments."

"Yes, you did seem like a stranger from another planet," Michael Barnes said. "I had a great deal of difficulty in understanding the language you were speaking, and it wasn't because of your French accent either! Your method of evaluating business success was entirely different from ours.

"Indeed it was," Monsieur St. Luc remembered, smiling at the thought of that long-ago meeting.

"How funny it seems now that we felt so far apart."

"Fred Smythe's goal at the meeting," Mr. Barnes began, "was to explain to Monsieur St. Luc our firm's philosophy, the process of analysis we used in evaluating a particular stock as an appropriate investment for a client.

"He explained that, in essence, a company's reported earnings and the expectation of future earnings growth was crucial to our evaluation of a common stock.

"He knew about the St. Luc vineyards, and he compared an investor's reasoning to that of a vineyard owner. The owner knows that by cultivating and caring for the vines, their yield and profitability will increase over time. In the same way, he said, investors should choose companies whose earnings will continually grow."

"This process of evaluation, of course, was not unique to our firm. Hundreds of thousands of other analysts and individual investors were doing the same thing every day, with varying degrees of success. Over time the market is very good at evaluating the earnings of each company and placing an accurate price on its common stock. Our job was to determine as accurately as possible, ahead of the market, the expectations for these earnings.

"Our goal was to do this better than anybody else, to identify those companies whose future earnings growth had not been fully recognized, and thus buy them at a good value.

"What the market is all about, he explained, was monitoring expectations of growth, trying to determine as accurately as possible, with as much information as possible, future earnings.

"We did this, he explained, not by trying to figure out where the "economy" was going, since nobody, including your St. Luc ancestors, ever knew with any real certainty where it was going. We did it, rather, by studying the trends of various industries, and the likely earnings growth of particular companies within those industries.

"Reliability of future earnings growth," he said, "was key. Knowing that Monsieur St. Luc had much experience in farming and grape culture, he used the examples of annual crops and grapes to explain the difference between unpredictable growth and predictable growth.

"Annual crops, he pointed out, are highly dependent on spring rains and good summer weather, resulting in a highly unpredictable product. The unpredictable nature of the weather and crop prices makes it very difficult to predict revenues and earnings from year to year.

"Grapes, on the other hand, which are planted once and which mature slowly over many years, produce a fairly predictable crop. They are not unaffected by weather, but as the vines mature and the reputation of the grape grows, as it did for Monsieur St. Luc's grapes, the future earnings of such a vineyard can be predicted with much greater accuracy.

"Identifying such predictable growth was the constant goal of a good securities analyst, he said. Sorting out all the information available about hundreds and thousands of companies, and making a price verdict based on their future earnings growth, was the analyst's job.

"It was then that the battle began, because Monsieur St. Luc said he wasn't going to put any of his money in company that he had to evaluate on the basis of future earnings growth.

"What he wanted to know, he said, was what the company's cash flow looked like."

"Yes, I made a pretty strong argument for cash flow," Monsieur St. Luc interjected. "Cash flow was a subject I understood. It was the management of cash flow that had allowed me to build the family business, not future earnings but the money l had in my hand.

"With that money I could go out and borrow more money, and that is exactly what my family and I had done so many times to expand the vineyard, build the winery, buy part-ownership in banks, build the resort.

"I took risks, and leveraged that money to make more money. Always, it was the amount of cash I was generating that determined what l could do next. Of course, my aim was always to build solid, profitable enterprises that would result in earnings down the road, but it wasn't the earnings that interested me. I didn't want to sell the businesses. I had no need to be concerned with their value day to day as profitable enterprises. What I needed to be concerned with was the amount of cash I had on hand to expand.

"If I was going to invest in other people's business by buying their common stock, l wanted to know what they were going to do with their cash flow.

"Your grandfather finally brought the two sides of the table together by explaining that being an entrepreneur and being an investor in a company were two different things.

"An entrepreneur," he said, "assumed large risks. He invited us all to walk over to the window and look down on two new buildings. In one you could see lights on in nearly all the office windows and people at work. The other, built at about the same time, was still sitting empty. Apparently, there were serious structural problems that developed during construction, and labor problems, and then the owner and builder had become locked in litigation, and by the time their dispute had been settled, and the building opened, the market for business tenants had softened. The owner of that building, it was obvious, was losing great sums of money, whereas the owner of the other building was making money.

"The risk, he noted, had to do with this very cash flow I was talking about. The entrepreneur puts his cash and borrowed money on the line, not knowing for certain whether the enterprise he is going to build will make money or not. When a project fails, like our watch factory, all is lost. When a project succeeds, like the resort, there are great rewards for the high risks that have been assumed.

"The investor in publicly owned companies, he said, assumed far less risk. He had the advantage of watching a company as it was founded, and as it began operating, and could wait to see if it would be successful or not. He had the advantage of being able to wait until an earnings pattern was visible. He didn't need to be concerned with how cash flow was going to be invested. What he was really judging was how past cash flow had been invested.

"The business owner, he noted, makes entrepreneurial decisions; the analyst makes investment decisions.

"The analyst judges the effectiveness of the entrepreneur's decisions long after they are made and have begun to show results translated into earnings.

"The entrepreneur manages a business, and should it fail, like the watch business, it cannot be easily liquidated. The analyst can move easily from one business to another.

"The entrepreneur has a narrow field of vision, focusing almost entirely on the running of the business. The analyst has a broad vision, and compares businesses across a broad spectrum of industries.

"The entrepreneur builds; the analyst judges."

"The analyst develops comparative knowledge; the analyst has the opportunity of placing the value on the end result or expectations of one entrepreneur's decisions versus another's.

"The entrepreneur assumes the greater risks and has the potential for the greater rewards. The analyst makes decisions where the results are more certain, and accepts both less risk and more limited rewards.

"He was convincing enough that I agreed that an entrepreneur's decision and an analyst's decision were two different things," Monsieur St. Luc said, "and that while cash flow mattered a lot to me in my business maybe it didn't have to matter so much to an investor."

And then Monsieur St. Luc said. "I did do much of the talking that day, didn't I?

"Because I had always been involved in private enterprise, and had never dealt with publicly owned businesses, my only concern had been private market value. I only cared what a piece of real estate or business was worth if l wanted to buy it or sell it.

"So the same question I asked of Fred Smythe, "how much are these companies that you are telling me to invest in worth on the private market? I know what their stock value is, but what would they be worth if a private individual went to buy the whole company?

"Fred said he didn't know, and that furthermore, he didn't think it mattered that if you could predict future earnings growth, you knew that a stock would continue to rise in price. What did it matter, he said, what its private market value was? As a stock investor, you needed to be concerned only with the public value of that stock."

"Of course you never quite know the private market value of anything until it is sold.

"Still, you can make some pretty good estimates, and when a company is sold, you do learn its precise private market value. That price can be used as a benchmark for potential sales of similar companies.

Many of the publicly traded companies in the US are worth more privately than they are traded for publicly, which means that their stocks are consistently undervalued. It became apparent that the reason for their greater private worth was that they could be bought more cheaply than they could be built today. By purchasing companies who use cash flow to pay down debt and support the companies growth, the buyer was making excellent use of the laws of leverage.

"We began looking for companies likely to be purchased, and whose private market value was higher than their publicly traded price. Using this selection criterion, we were assured that we were paying less for a company than it could be built anew or bought privately.

"In this way, we were buying ownership in a company at a double discount, and with a big built-in safety factor. If a company can be bought privately for less than it would cost to build it from scratch all over again, and if at that price it can support additional debt and still produce significant profits for the buyer, then purchasing a share of stock in the open market at a substantial discount to the private market value is an even safer investment. And no leveraging is required.

"Our firm had for some time held substantial amounts of stock in a small well-run newspaper chain whose earnings growth had been steady over many years and was expected to continue. We had never paid attention to its private market value, but then it was purchased by a large family-owned chain and overnight its stock value increased by 50 percent.

"This was the proof of Monsieur St. Luc's insistence that private market value did matter! We had attained our 'Ph.D.' in finance. Now, for the first time, we truly understood how a company is valued in the private market. From this point forward we analyzed every investment from both its open market or earnings potential and its private market or cash flow potential.

"Overall, we discovered that many companies were great long term investments while at the same time they were take over candidates at private marker values which turned out to be about one-third higher than it's stock market value.

"If so many stocks are such a bargain, why do some people lose money in the market?" Julie asked.

"Many people who lose money in the market are people who don't understand that price volatility, the up and down movement of stock prices, is not directly related to the long-term worth of the company, to its expected earnings growth, or its private market value," Michael Barnes replied. "They are the people who buy a stock and then sell it three or six months later in panic because it has temporarily gone down in value. What they should be looking at is the company itself, the fundamentals that led them to purchase it in the first place, not the market's day to day fluctuations. If you have invested in companies whose future earnings growth seems assured, you'll do well if you stick with them if their prospects remain healthy. If you focus your attention on the strengths and weaknesses of companies and industries, and ignore the up and down movements of the market you will come out well ahead in the long run. Volatility, or price fluctuations, are not the same thing as risk.

"This has been my experience over many years in the market," Mr. Barnes said.

"My clients who have taken the long view have enjoyed a steady increase in the value of their assets and income over time."

"What I hear you telling Paul and me and Mme. Nadolsky is that putting our money in publicly owned companies is the soundest way we can assure our financial futures, Julie said. "Monsieur St. Luc has demonstrated persuasively the growth in assets that can come from productive private enterprise. We have seen that the hard work of clearing land and nurturing grapevines on a small plot was the beginning of substantial assets for the St. Luc family. We see clearly now that from the most modest beginnings one can build wealth over time. It is exactly what Paul's grandfather wanted us to see firsthand, I am sure. There's no better time to learn such a lesson than at our stage in life. But stocks? I don't know.

"If you look at the performance of the various forms of investment available to the person who doesn't want to assume the risk and energy involved in managing a company or real estate investments themselves, then stocks are by far the safest and best investments available," Michael Barnes said.

"That may have been true when you were young and when Paul's grandfather was younger," Julie said, "but the world is a different place today. The U.S. has gone from becoming the world's biggest lender to its biggest debtor. We're in trouble! What about our federal trade deficit? For some years now we've been spending far more on imports than we sell in exports."

"These are in the nature of political challenges," Michael Barnes said, "and there have always been political challenges. In my view, they should not affect your decision to invest in America's companies. Productive enterprise has a life of its own, quite separate from the political arena, and it always has. As Monsieur St. Luc would surely agree, you can't harvest what you don't plant.

"If you want to consider instability and trouble, think of all the enormous tragedies and difficulties of the past half-century: World War II, the Korean War, the Vietnam War, assassinations, terrorism, natural disasters. Such events as the Arab oil embargo of 1973 and the prime rate hitting 21 percent in 1980 were also major crises from a financial standpoint. There are literally hundreds, thousands, of serious crises, large and small, which have consumed the world in our lifetimes. It is certain they will continue to do so. But through these difficulties, business enterprise has continued to be productive and has grown. And those people who invested in that enterprise have seen their assets and income grow as well, through good times and bad.

"As long as there are people like Paul's grandfather and Monsieur St. Luc who develop products and services that make the world a better place, there will be profitable enterprises," Michael Barnes said. "The world, no matter how many difficulties it may face, never runs out of the need for good products and good services. It is those needs that fuel the marketplace, and as long as there is human need there will be productivity and growth."

"What I hear you saying is that there are substantial rewards for the person who can learn to live with volatility," Julie said.

"Indeed, I am," Michael Barnes said. "If you look at the ups and downs of publicly trades stocks as compared to the overall trend over time, you will see that short-term volatility can be of no significance," he said. "It is simply something that you must live with as a stock investor. It has virtually unrelated to long term. Risk comes from investing in a bad company, or from putting all your money into fixed income investments, where you have no protection from inflation. Volatility is different from risk. It is merely the response of the market to each day's activity, and it has little effect on the ultimate worth of the companies in which you are investing. If they are good companies, their earnings will keep growing and their prices will follow.

"Whenever the market's ups and downs seem risky to you, remember the crucial difference between preserving your capital and preserving your purchasing power. With fixed-income investments, which generally reflect the rate of inflation plus about two percent, you can usually preserve your dollars. But what are those dollars worth when you go to buy something? Once you deduct inflation and taxes, your returns if any, are nominal.

"It might be helpful to remember that there are three risks and two rewards in any investment. The risks are inflation, taxes and capital loss. The rewards are appreciation and income. These five factors should be weighed, relative to the time frame of an investment decision.

"On a very short-term basis, say one year, inflation and taxes are rather inconsequential. Capital loss is a factor.

"Over time, the weight of evidence shifts. Inflation and taxes are near certainties, and their negative effect on investment returns is very measurable. Ironically, the possibility of capital loss, that which investors fear the most, virtually disappears the longer the investment horizon stretches out. By the same token, capital appreciation becomes a near certainty with time. Increased investment income from ownership of business is as equally certain as capital appreciation with time. Only ownership of business enterprise offers protection of your purchasing power. Your only concern as a stock investor should be to find good companies and to keep an eye on them to see if they retain their good qualities.

"If you look at investment returns of the market over the last century, you will find that the average stock has attained a 11 percent return annually, including dividends. This compares to bonds yielding 6% and an underlying inflation of 3%. We refer to this as our 11/6/3 guideline, which we will come back to. But it's important to remember that the rime horizon for the average investor is somewhere in the area of 25 years and that long-term returns are what you want to look for when you are selecting a manager to help you manage your assets."

"Ok," Paul said. "How do you make those choices?"

"Here's how we do it," Michael Barnes said. "We use five keys. The first two are near-term considerations, in line with the philosophy of my old mentor Frederick Smythe:

"1) The relative strength of the stock, or what we call 'market leadership'.

"Stocks go up and down for a reason. The market is smart and moves on the basis of information. So, we ask why is a stock going up? Why is a stock going down? Usually there are reasons that can be discovered if one does enough homework. Usually stocks, which are increasing in price ahead of the market, are doing so because the expectations of their earnings have increased. Conversely, those that decline do so for the opposite reason. By paying attention to those movements, we can focus our research on those companies that deserve our closest attention at any given time.

"2) The worth of earnings momentum over the next 2-3 years.

"There are points in time when a company's stock is most attractively priced relative to its immediate earnings expectations and relative to other companies in other industries. This is where our comparative knowledge pays off. We look for companies whose earnings will grow by 50 percent or more over the next 2-3 years, and we use our comparative knowledge to identify which of these companies are selling for less than their earnings growth indicates they are worth. We are quantifying a company's future value in the public market."

At that point Paul interjected a question. "You have told us that we should view our stock investments as a long-term undertaking. But the points you have just made have to do with shorter-term considerations. Are you contradicting yourself?"

"Not really." Michael Barnes said. "You could actually ignore these steps and still get an average return from your investments over time, a return that will outshine all fixed-return investments. Like the vine, your investments would continue to grow and yield rewards.

"But the great advantage of stock investments is that they do give you the opportunity to make comparisons among companies, and to go with those that show the greatest potential for growth. Your overall focus should always be on the long term, but for enhanced returns you must make adjustments over shorter periods of time."

"3) Private market value.

"This is the one that Monsieur St. Luc likes so much. It entails the analysis of the current cash flow of a company, and the determination of its current private market value. If a company is being publicly traded for less than it's worth privately, it is undervalued, especially if there is a chance it will be bought out. Many of our investments are in stocks selling significantly below their private market value. Between the analysis of future earnings and current cash flow, we are assessing the current as well as the future value of the stock.

"4) Proprietary nature of the company.

"We like companies with products or services which set them apart from other companies, something that makes them special and gives them protection from competition, like the St. Luc grapevines. Such companies are likely to enjoy protected earning growth over a very long time.

"5) The elusive judgment call.

"I have told you that we look at market leadership, public and private market values and that we search for proprietary businesses. But no company has all these characteristics in equal proportion. Judgment demands that we decide which of these components are the most important at any given time.

"The other important part of judgment, which can come only from long experience, is the decision to sell. This decision probably requires more knowledge and greater experience than any other. When it comes to selling, you are always operating in a knowledge vacuum because the investment world doesn't publicize negatives. And yet the best sell decisions are made by uncovering negative change. We constantly look for changes that could negatively impact either the public or private market value of the companies we own.

"Recognizing negative changes gives us our greatest single method of protecting capital. We sell a stock in response to negative change, and put the cash reserves for the short term in fixed-income securities or money market funds. These reserves are held until a suitable new investment can be found. This one step can go a long way toward reducing overall volatility and protecting capital during adverse market conditions since negative change often precedes market declines.

"As I mentioned earlier, open market common stock investments have returned an average annual return of 11 percent over the past half-century. Our goal, by faithfully following our investment philosophy, is to exceed this 11 percent.

"But how does all of this apply to Paul and me, or to Mme. Nadolsky?" Julie asked. "We're at very different stages in our lives."

"If you look at all the factors we use to judge a company, there is only one that I would weigh differently for the young person and the retiree, and that is cash flow," Michael Barnes answered.

"For the young person, a company that is using all of its cash flow plus additional debt to support its growth can be a wise choice. There are many companies, which haven't come close to exhausting their potential growth. A business making continued new investments for expansion is the classic definition of a growth company, and the best investment choice for you and Paul.

"For Mme. Nadolsky and any retiree, solid companies with significant free cash flow are the single safest investment they can find. Essentially, free cash flow is reported earnings plus depreciation minus capital expenditures.

'The company with free cash flow is a maturing company, usually with limited debt. It is like the mature grapevine…it keeps on producing a substantial yield even though it was planted many years earlier. The stocks of such companies will go up and down in price, like all other stocks, but they provide relatively assured returns in the long term.

"Free cash flow is like a dividend, and should be considered so. Whether it's distributed to the shareholders or not, they will benefit from its ultimate value, whether through acquisitions, expansion, retirement of debt or repurchase of the company's own stock. Free cash flow companies are prime takeover candidates."

"But what's the long term?" Mme. Nadolsky asked. I'm already 65 years old, you know."

"As Monsieur St. Luc pointed out, people who reach the age of 65 are likely, from an actuarial standpoint, to live for another 20 years," said Michael Barnes. "Considering your good health and the advances in medicine, it could easily be 30 years for you. That's very long term by any standard of investment.

"People often misunderstand life expectancy tables," he continued. "Life expectancy for a newborn today is about 72 for women. But those life expectancies change as we grow older. The fact that you have survived increases your chances of longevity, statistically speaking. As a 65-year-oldJ you probably have a life expectancy of 85 or more."

"Oh, I hope so," Mme. Nadolsky said.

"Understanding life expectancy is important in being able to judge the duration of your investment decisions. When you get to be 65, you may feel as though you are nearing the end of your life and your involvement with investments. But in truth you are closer to the beginning of your investment life. Now is when your investment decisions will really matter. You no longer have the protection of earned income to cover your mistakes."

"I see it is approaching noon, may I suggest we stroll over to our favorite restaurant." concluded Michael.

Chapter 15

Harvesting Capital

"Is this it?" Paul asked Monsieur St. Lucas they enjoyed their glasses of wine while waiting for lunch to be served. "Have we learned the lessons we were sent to learn? This gathering feels somehow like a graduation party.

"If it feels so, it must mean you have learned enough to be confident of your own future," he smiled.

"Yes, I really do," said Paul. "There's nothing like seeing things up close. Working on the farm and in the vineyard, going to Glacier Pointe, I have many images that will always help me remember the rewards of human enterprise."

"Observe and learn," Julie said. "We have observed and we have learned. I won't forget what your grandfather and his brothers wrote on the barn wall."

"Most of all, remember the vine," Paul said. "That's the one we will always return to. Whenever we feel impatient, overworked or confused about an investment, we will remember the vine."

"To the vine!" Mme. Nadolsky said with great cheer. "Its lessons are good for a lifetime; I am convinced once and for all. There is no time in your life, ever, when you can afford to stop being a part of productive enterprise."

"Well said!" Monsieur St. Luc raised his glass in compliment to Mme. Nadolsky's good investment sense, and then toasted everyone all around the table.

"There's just one more lesson to think about, Michael Barnes said. "Monsieur St. Luc and I, as you have seen, view investments from quite different perspectives. But we are in total agreement that ownership of business is essential to good investing. He is living proof that entrepreneurship can create great wealth. For my part, I can vouch for the fact that owning businesses by investing in publicly traded companies is a path to long-term reward. Monsieur St. Luc will go on being an entrepreneur for the rest of his days. He's never going to stop working, if he can help it. He'll always be earning income. Am I right, Monsieur St. Luc?"

"Absolutely," Monsieur St. Luc laughed.

"And if you couldn't work because of illness, your assets are more than sufficient to take care of you for many, many years, right?

"Yes, I've been blessed with abundance," Monsieur St. Luc agreed.

"Most people," Michael Barnes continued, "aren't Monsieur St. Luc. They don't have the experience of being an entrepreneur and they don't have the capital to effectively ignore risk. Their life history is usually something like this: When they are Paul and Julie's ages, they begin saving, and when they have enough for a down payment, they buy a starter home, employing leverage. For the next 25 years or so, their expenses, as a percentage of their earned income, are high, making planned savings quite difficult. They have house payments, and all the expenses

connected with raising children and living a life: furniture, automobiles, education and on and on.

"Then, all of a sudden, at age 50 or so their circumstances change. The mortgage is paid off, or nearly so; the children have graduated from college or otherwise have become independent. It is during this time, from about 50 until they stop working, that they accumulate most of their assets for investing. Their earnings continue moving upward while their spending goes down. If they're fortunate, they may also have retirement plan assets that have been building for many years.

"At that point they are in the position Mme. Nadolsky is now in: they have a paid-for home, investments and a retirement plan. They have the same goals as those people living on Villette Strasse or Amden Strasse. They want to remain comfortable even though they are no longer going to earn income.

"This is the point at which they need to review their assets in relation to future income needs. If they take their annual income needs and add taxes and inflation and compare those costs with the assets they have available for investing, they can approximate the rate of return they will need to meet all of their needs without spending their underlying assets. For some people, the rate of return required will be so high as to be unattainable. These people will have to continue working on their goals and learn to live with less. Others will be more fortunate.

"The best of all possible worlds, of course, is to have enough capital to sustain yourself regardless of future circumstances.

"How do you figure out how much capital is enough capital? We suggest an analysis of your net worth that takes into consideration the following factors:

"First: Your annual income needs. Be realistic and don't forget to factor in an annual increase for inflation, perhaps by 3 percent per year, over the course of your life expectancy.

"Second: Don't think of the house or condominium or apartment that you live in as an investment. Think of it as an asset. Most people wish to remain in their residence indefinitely- and while they're there they'll be paying property taxes, homeowner's insurance, and all the other costs associated with maintaining a home. An investment, by contrast, should produce income rather than be an income drain. This doesn't mean that your residence won't increase in value over time. It probably will. But not as much as you might think. Studies show that home values increase at a rate something less than inflation.

"You could, of course, sell your residence it if you needed the money, but your goal should be for other investments to produce enough income to support you and your residence.

"Third: Do an inventory of your investments- what they're worth now; what you paid for them --and be mindful of any debts you may have.

"Fourth: Maintain a healthy respect for history. Remember the 11/6/3 guideline. For nearly a century stocks have averaged an annual return of 11%, appreciation plus dividends, while bonds have yielded 6%. This was in a mildly inflationary environment of 3% annually. The past, of course, is not necessarily the future. But history always teaches us lessons and shouldn't be ignored.

"Fifth: Never forget taxes. Every country has its own form of taxation. Switzerland has a 35% income tax with no capital gains tax while the US has an income tax graduatal to nearly 50% with a capital gains rate of 20%.

"In addition, many Americans have retirement assets which can be rolled over into Individual Retirement Accounts (IRAs). How you divide your investments between stocks (in which you're looking for capital appreciation) and bonds (in which you're looking for income) and whether you hold those investments in regular accounts or tax deferred accounts (such as IRAs), can affect your tax bite and thus your overall returns.

"And last: Balance: Most pension funds have about 65 percent of their assets invested in stocks and about 35 percent of their assets invested in bonds. For most people going into their retirement years, this is a pretty reasonable balance.

"It's true that bonds can never be expected to provide as high a return as stocks. But stocks, even the best of them, can fall in value by 15 percent or more at any time, and often do. In a dramatic market downturn, which will occur from time to time, they may lose nearly half their value! (In the 1973-74 plunge, stocks lost 45% of their value on average.) Not many retirees can sleep well at night knowing that they could wake up in the morning with a portfolio worth half the value it had been when they went to bed the night before. Bonds are a good antidote to such depressing possibilities. They don't prevent a portfolio from losing some of its value, but they can usually limit the slide to 15 or 20 percent.

"But giving up some of the potential upside of stocks by putting a third of your portfolio or more in bonds, you gain a more acceptable level of volatility and the promise of more peaceful dreams." Michael paused and took a sip from his wine glass.

"I can see Monsieur St. Luc giving me that glance of his," he said. "I know what he wants to say and he's right, of course. All right, say it, Monsieur St. Luc!"

Monsieur St. Luc laughed. "Michael, you know me too well." he said. "I think it's the philosopher in me. I just have to keep reminding myself and all of us that life doesn't provide many absolutes. There are few guarantees and many unknowns. Much is unpredictable.

"Some of the glory and the mystery of life derives from these very unknowns. But most of us would prefer not to have our food and clothing and shelter and other comforts of life be unpredictable. We want to be able to count on those things. And that's why I like your approach to a balanced portfolio, Michael That's why I wanted you to talk to us today."

"There's just one more thing to think about in this whole business of moving from a life where you earn an income to one in which you live off of your investments," Michael continued. "I know that Monsieur St. Luc showed you a chart that demonstrates what will happen to your investments over time if you depend entirely on bonds- if you expect bonds producing, for instance, a six percent income to support your needs if those needs require a six percent return on your investments. You would think that such a match would work, but it doesn't. Over time your assets shrink quite dramatically.

"Is there another way to get that six percent return?

"While as Monsieur St. Luc just said, there are few guarantees in life, there are ways to diminish your risk considerably.

"Let me show you a chart in which we'll assume that you're entering your retirement with $1 million in assets and you estimate that your annual income needs are $60,000. (This number, remember, will go up each year because of inflation.)

"If we set up a portfolio modeled after the typical pension fund (65% in common stocks, 35% in bonds, and if we assume an 11 percent annual return from the stock market, a six percent annual return from the bond market and an inflation rate of three per cent, and if we assume you'll be taxed at a rate of 20% on your capital gains and 30% on your income from your bonds, what do we get?"

"As you see, the news is pretty good. After 25 years, by which time you're 90 years old, you still have nearly $400,000 in assets and you haven't had to reduce your standard of living at all over the years. Here's how it works:

Portfolio Distribution of 6% per Year

	At Beginning of Year	Gain 9.25%	Paid 25%	Needs	At End of Year
Year 1	$1,000,000	$92,500	$(23,125)	$(60,000)	$1,009,375
Year 2	$1,009,375	$93,367	$(23,342)	$(61,800)	$1,017,600
Year 3	$1,017,600	$94,128	$(23,532)	$(63,654)	$1,024,542
Year 4	$1,024,542	$94,770	$(23,693)	$(65,564)	$1,030,056
Year 5	$1,030,055	$95,280	$(23,820)	$(67,531)	$1,033,986
Year 6	$1,033,986	$95,644	$(23,911)	$(69,556)	$1,036,162
Year 7	$1,036,162	$95,845	$(23,961)	$(71,643)	$1,036,403
Year 8	$1,036,403	$95,867	$(23,967)	$(73,792)	$1,034,511
Year 9	$1,034,511	$95,692	$(23,923)	$(76,006)	$1,030,274
Year 10	$1,030,274	$95,300	$(23,825)	$(78,286)	$1,023,463
Year 11	$1,023,463	$94,670	$(23,668)	$(80,635)	$1,013,831
Year 12	$1,013,830	$93,779	$(23,445)	$(83,054)	$1,001,111
Year 13	$1,001,110	$92,603	$(23,151)	$(85,546)	$985,018
Year 14	$985,016	$91,114	$(22,779)	$(88,112)	$965,241
Year 15	$965,241	$89,285	$(22,321)	$(90,755)	$941,449
Year 16	$941,450	$87,084	$(21,771)	$(93,478)	$913,284
Year 17	$913,285	$84,479	$(21,120)	$(96,282)	$880,361
Year 18	$880,362	$81,433	$(20,358)	$(99,171)	$842,265
Year 19	$842,266	$77,910	$(19,478)	$(102,146)	$798,551
Year 20	$798,552	$73,866	$(18,467)	$(105,210)	$748,741
Year 21	$748,741	$69,259	$(17,315)	$(108,367)	$692,318
Year 22	$692,318	$64,039	$(16,010)	$(111,618)	$628,730
Year 23	$628,729	$58,157	$(14,539)	$(114,966)	$557,382
Year 24	$557,381	$51,558	$(12,890)	$(118,415)	$477,635
Year 25	$477,634	$44,181	$(11,045)	$(121,968)	$388,803

"Column two shows the amount of return, assuming an average return of 9.25% (based on your 65%-35% stock-bond mix.)

"Column three shows how much you will pay in taxes per year using a combination of capital gains rate and income tax rates.

"Column four shows your $60,000 initial income requirement, and its increase over time because of inflation. "In column five you see that your principal will decline but not run out at least not in the first 25 years!

"I've brought two more charts. They demonstrate how spending less of your income can, not surprisingly, leave you with a great deal more!

"In the chart we just looked at, you were spending at the rate of six percent of your annual return on your assets. Suppose you only spent five per cent? Or four per cent? The results below show you the dramatic difference, assuming everything else remains the same.

Portfolio Distribution of 5% per Year

	At Beginning of Year	Gain 9.25%	Paid 25%	Needs	At End of Year
Year 1	$1,000,000	$92,500	$(23,125)	$(50,000)	$1,019,375
Year 2	$1,019,375	$94,292	$(23,573)	$(51,500)	$1,038,594
Year 3	$1,038,594	$96,070	$(24,017)	$(53,045)	$1,057,602
Year 4	$1,057,602	$97,828	$(24,457)	$(54,636)	$1,076,336
Year 5	$1,076,336	$99,561	$(24,890)	$(56,275)	$1,094,732
Year 6	$1,094,732	$101,263	$(25,316)	$(57,964)	$1,112,715
Year 7	$1,112,715	$102,926	$(25,732)	$(59,703)	$1,130,207
Year 8	$1,130,207	$104,544	$(26,136)	$(61,494)	$1,147,121
Year 9	$1,147,121	$106,109	$(26,527)	$(63,339)	$1,163,364
Year 10	$1,163,365	$107,611	$(26,903)	$(65,239)	$1,178,834
Year 11	$1,178,834	$109,042	$(27,261)	$(67,196)	$1,193,420
Year 12	$1,193,420	$110,391	$(27,598)	$(69,212)	$1,207,002
Year 13	$1,207,002	$111,648	$(27,912)	$(71,288)	$1,219,450
Year 14	$1,219,450	$112,799	$(28,200)	$(73,427)	$1,230,622
Year 15	$1,230,622	$113,833	$(28,458)	$(75,629)	$1,240,367
Year 16	$1,240,367	$114,734	$(28,683)	$(77,898)	$1,248,519
Year 17	$1,248,519	$115,488	$(28,872)	$(80,235)	$1,254,900
Year 18	$1,254,900	$116,078	$(29,020)	$(82,642)	$1,259,316
Year 19	$1,259,316	$116,487	$(29,122)	$(85,122)	$1,261,560
Year 20	$1,261,560	$116,694	$(29,174)	$(87,675)	$1,261,405
Year 21	$1,261,405	$116,680	$(29,170)	$(90,306)	$1,258,610
Year 22	$1,258,610	$116,421	$(29,105)	$(93,015)	$1,252,911
Year 23	$1,252,911	$115,894	$(28,974)	$(95,805)	$1,244,026
Year 24	$1,244,026	$115,072	$(28,768)	$(98,679)	$1,231,651
Year 25	$1,231,651	$113,928	$(28,482)	$(101,640)	$1,215,458

Portfolio Distribution of 4% per Year

	At Beginning of Year	Gain 9.25%	Paid 25%	Needs	At End of Year
Year 1	$1,000,000	$92,500	$(23,125)	$(40,000)	$1,029,375
Year 2	$1,029,375	$95,217	$(23,804)	$(41,200)	$1,059,588
Year 3	$1,059,588	$98,012	$(24,503)	$(42,436)	$1,090,661
Year 4	$1,090,661	$100,886	$(25,222)	$(43,709)	$1,122,616
Year 5	$1,122,616	$103,842	$(25,961)	$(45,020)	$1,155,477
Year 6	$1,155,477	$106,882	$(26,720)	$(46,371)	$1,189,268
Year 7	$1,189,268	$110,007	$(27,502)	$(47,762)	$1,224,011
Year 8	$1,224,011	$113,221	$(28,305)	$(49,195)	$1,259,732
Year 9	$1,259,732	$116,525	$(29,131)	$(50,671)	$1,296,455
Year 10	$1,296,455	$119,922	$(29,981)	$(52,191)	$1,344,206
Year 11	$1,334,206	$123,414	$(30,854)	$(53,757)	$1,373,010
Year 12	$1,373,010	$127,003	$(31,751)	$(55,369)	$1,412,893
Year 13	$1,412,893	$130,693	$(32,673)	$(57,030)	$1,453,882
Year 14	$1,453,882	$134,484	$(33,621)	$(58,741)	$1,496,003
Year 15	$1,496,003	$138,380	$(34,595)	$(60,504)	$1,539,285
Year 16	$1,539,285	$142,384	$(35,596)	$(62,319)	$1,583,754
Year 17	$1,583,754	$146,497	$(36,624)	$(64,188)	$1,629,439
Year 18	$1,629,439	$150,723	$(37,681)	$(66,114)	$1,676,367
Year 19	$1,676,367	$155,064	$(38,766)	$(68,097)	$1,724,568
Year 20	$1,724,568	$159,523	$(39,881)	$(70,140)	$1,774,070
Year 21	$1,774,070	$164,101	$(41,025)	$(72,244)	$1,824,901
Year 22	$1,824,901	$168,803	$(42,201)	$(74,412)	$1,877,092
Year 23	$1,877,092	$173,631	$(43,408)	$(76,644)	$1,930,671
Year 24	$1,930,671	$178,587	$(44,647)	$(78,943)	$1,985,668
Year 25	$1,985,668	$183,674	$(45,919)	$(81,312)	$2,042,112

"As you can see, reducing the annual income to a five per cent payout allows you to maintain the value of your portfolio indefinitely. The last chart reduces income to 4% per year. The benefit is that the ending estate will be identical to today, adjusted for inflation.

"That's why we recommend to our clients that they strive for an income payout between four and five percent. By doing so they should have sufficient assets and income for almost any circumstance.

"People, like Mms. Nadolsky, who are entering the retirement phase of their lives mustn't forget about estate planning either- what you want to have happen to your assets after you're gone. Tax law is complex and it's a good idea to review your options every couple of years or as your circumstances change.

"Thank you for these wonderful charts," Mme. Nadolsky said. "They tell me that I am going to be just fine- and they're a reminder to spend carefully, just as I always have."

"This has been a terrific review," offered Monsieur St. Lucas their food arrived at the table.

"Yes it has," said Julie. "It's a good reminder to people like me who are just starting out on life's journey to always think ahead. I'm so glad you thought ahead, Mme. Nadolsky."

"I never quite realized how happy I'd feel about my careful planning until this moment," Mme. Nadolsky said. "I was always aiming for security, for peace of mind, and now I think I have achieved it. Thank you, Michael, for showing me the future!"

She smiled a slightly wicked grin. "And you, Monsieur St. Luc, for reminding me that the future can never be quite known and that I must always enjoy each day as it comes along."

Chapter 16
The Envelopes

"There's just one more thing," Paul said after they had finished their meal.

"Remember those three envelopes that my grandfather gave me? He wrote in his letter that I would know what to do with them when the time came. I'm certain now is the time!"

"Do you have them with you?'! Monsieur St. Luc asked.

Paul pulled the three envelopes from inside coat pocket and put them on the table.

"Yes, I sure do. I've been afraid to leave them anywhere for fear I'd lose them."

"Oh, this is exciting," Mme. Nadolsky said. "I love mysteries. What do you suppose is in them?"

"If it's shares of some of your grandfather's best stocks, you'll be sitting pretty," Michael Barnes laughed.

"I'm sure it's nothing like that," Paul said. "Grandfather believes that young people should work for their money, that the pride of accomplishment is priceless. I'm sure it's something he considers even more valuable than such a gift.

"Well, we'll soon know," he said, and handed Julie the first envelope. "You've been as curious as I. Open the first one!"

Julie took the first envelope, which was now considerably wrinkled from all the time it had spent in Paul's coat pocket. They had felt something inside it, but they couldn1t quite figure out what it was. Many was the time they'd fingered it since the morning after their wedding, trying to imagine what it might be. But its true identity was unknowable until now.

"Whatever is in these envelopes Grandfather considered them

important," Paul said. "I'm sure that's why he asked us to wait until now to open them. He knew that our interest would be piqued by the wait. He has a finely developed sense of the dramatic, which is of course why he sent us on this trip in the first place."

Julie ripped open the envelope and out onto the table fell the dried tendril of grapevine. "Remember the vine," she laughed. That's how we're to remember the vine, isn't it? We'll have to have it framed and hang it in the living room, whenever we have a living room, that is. I think your grandfather has a sense of humor along with his sense of drama."

"He definitely does," Michael Barnes said. "That's one of the reasons I enjoy working with him as a client. It helps to have a sense of humor when you're trying to remember that volatility and risk are not the same thing, that even the stocks of good companies can take a temporary downturn."

"Let's see what else is in the envelopes," Monsieur St. Luc said.

"I think I'll open this other bumpy one," Paul said. "We think it has a key in it, but we can't figure out what key."

"The key to your future!" Mme. Nadolsky said, getting into the spirit of the occasion.

Paul opened the envelope and indeed, inside was a single key, which fell loudly to the table.

"Does it have anything written on it?" Mme. Nadolsky inquired. Paul handed her the key to examine more closely. "It's just an ordinary key," she said. "I can't imagine what your grandfather intended by sending you across the ocean with a lockless key."

"Wait," Julie said. "I think there's a piece of paper in the envelope, too." She pulled out the handwritten note and read it aloud. "One of the great pleasures of having money is being able to share your good fortune with others. Wealth is worth nothing unless it is matched with a spirit of sharing. This key represents the key to your starter home, for which I shall provide the down payment."

She and Paul both jumped up at the same time and hugged each other as everybody else around the table clapped for them. "I can't believe it!" Julie beamed. "It's so wonderful."

"It's everything we hoped for," Paul said. "But of course it's just the sort of thing Grandfather would think of. It doesn't deprive us of our responsibilities, but it gives us a great boost in getting started."

"Just as the family farm provided the small amount of capital I needed to get started," Monsieur St. Luc said, "and just as scholarship money allowed your grandfather to get the education he wanted so badly. There is still a third envelope," he reminded them. "Don't forget that one."

"Here, Mme. Nadolsky, you open it." Paul said. "You've been an important part of our learning experiences here, and you should have the pleasure of opening the third envelope."

Mme. Nadolsky opened the third envelope with great delicacy, taking her time as she unglued the flap carefully and winked mischievously at the others. "This is the last envelope," she said. "I don't want the fun to end too soon." In her envelope was a large piece of heavy parchment paper beautifully inscribed in an experienced calligraphic hand. "Oh, how gorgeous," she exclaimed. "This, too, will have to be framed and hung in your living room, so that you will always remember us and all that you learned here. These things you now know so well, as do we all."

And she read the following:
- "There is no substitute for hard work.
- "Learn from your failures; persevere.
- "Observe and Learn.
- "Respect the laws of leverage.
- "Patience and time are an investor's greatest allies.
- "Understand cash flow and earnings.
- "Make inflation work for you --always.
- "Remember the vine."

The 25-Year Vision of
REMEMBER THE VINE

Chapter 17

The 2016 St. Luc Investment Seminar at Glacier Pointe

It was over 25 years ago that Paul and Julie returned from Switzerland. Upon Paul's return to the United State, he made a career decision to become an investment manager. He started by receiving an MBA degree in finance and then applied to, and was hire by, the Smythe Investment Company. He began his career there by verifying past investment information. The purpose of this verification was to identify how past investment strategies taken 25 years ago, or earlier, either succeeded or failed.

For nearly 10 years, Paul collected bits and pieces of information which when put together produced a high quality, high growth rate common stock portfolio which was specifically designed for the taxable investor. The firm thought so much about it that they asked Paul to run a division of the company that dealt exclusively with what became the Smythe Portfolio. Because the Smythe Portfolio was so successful, Paul was asked to become the research director for the Smythe Investment Company.

These are Paul's credentials and why he was asked to be the seminar's speaker.

The concept of realistic long-term investing and maintaining patience remain as valid today as they did twenty-five years ago. However, the specifics of how to invest for the long-term have changed. And that's what this seminar is all about, to present a very straight-forward thought process for a taxable investor with at least $1,000,000 to successfully invest.

Each piece of investment strategy is presented in chapter form. And each chapter will state "take away" points, verify what is stated and provide a brief summary. When all the chapters and points are put together, you will have a very structured investment philosophy.

One more point. Paul is very straightforward and he will pull no punches.

May the seminar begin.

Chapter 18

The Beginning of Verification.
Life Expectancy, Compounding and the Permanent Vision

M y name is Paul Crutcher and I would first like to thank you all for attending the St. Luc Seminar here at this beautiful resort, the Chalet at Glacier Pointe. Frankly, I am honored to be your guest speaker this morning. My hope is that each of you will walk away today with a much better understanding of how to properly invest your savings for the long run.

Take Away

Understanding the vital importance that time can play in growing your money, what else should you, as an investor, be cognizant of when beginning to think about investing for the long term? Well, at my firm we believe that two of the answers to that question are **life expectancy** and **compounding**. In fact, not only do these serve as a great starting point, they also can be found at the core of our firm's total investment philosophy, which we call the permanent vision.

Verification

Let's take a look at a few verification tables to dive deeper into what I am talking about. First is expected future life expectance:

Couples' Current Age	Surviving Spouse's Age at Death	Years to Live
65	92	27
75	94	18
85	96	11

The final column of that chart—years to live—is what I want to draw your attention to for a moment. Most investors, particularly those who are 65 years, or older, don't realize that their future life expectancy is 27 years. Nor do they understand how much $1,000,000 dollars can be worth when compounding for various periods of time or at different rates. As a result, when they reach the age of 65, they tend to think in short terms. Let's construct that table (later we will show you how expenses affect these numbers):

$1,000,000 Investable Assets			
	Expected Rate of Return		
Life Expectancy	5%	7.5%	10%
11 years	$1,710,000	$2,215,000	$2,853,000
18 years	$2,406,000	$3,676,000	$5,560,000
27 years	$3,733,000	$7,047,000	$13,110,000

These numbers are worth a second look. What you are seeing here is the magic of *time* and *compounding* at work. And while these calculations are not hard to work out, many people do not properly take these into account when making decisions about their money and retirement.

To further this point about the power of *time* and *compounding*, let me turn to a report that was written at the end of 2014. This report takes us back a half- century, to the end of 1964, and works its way forward. From that date, we actually have two twenty-five year periods of time: 1964—1989 and 1990—2015. We know from our research that for the first twenty-five years that the S&P 500 Index produced a total compounded annual rate of return of 10.02%. And for the most recent twenty-five years that return was 9.49%.

Pretty consistent, wouldn't you say?

Although the returns for those two periods were very consistent the circumstances were rather inconsistent. There were wars, recessions, bubbles, and on and on. They never stop. Take, for example, interest rates. It is commonly believed that as interest rates go down, stocks go up, and vice versa. That may be true on a shorter-term basis, but over the past two twenty-five year periods interest rates on 10-year government bonds did the following:

From 1964 through 1989 rates nearly doubled, from 4.2% to 8%.

From 1989 through 2014, however, rates went from 8% to 2.2%— down over 70%. Interest rates are a powerful factor in the economy and, therefore, it would be logical to assume that there would be an effect on investment returns during those same two timeframes. But, if there was an effect it was negligible. And this would be true of any other factor one can think of. Why?

If you would examine just one piece of the S&P 500 it nearly tells the whole story. For both twenty-five year periods, the earnings of the S&P increased fivefold. When you combine this with free cash flow and dividends it produces a powerful force which absolutely dwarfs the so-called negative influences.

And that's just one piece of the driving forces that affect growth. Think about population growth, bigger and bigger GDP, incredible innovations, productivity gains, leverage, increases in wages and inflation. They all increased with time. The certainty of these factors absolutely overwhelms short-term thinking. In fact, we'll show how a one-year projected rate of return on common stocks will be achieved one- third of the time, while a twenty-five-year expected return (of near 10%) will be achieved over 90% of the time. How, you might ask? It's all due to the magic of compounding over time.

Summary

So, once again, the magic of **time** and **compounding** are a vital element in our investment philosophy. In the coming chapters, I will build on this with other critical pieces to this investment strategy for turning your $1,000,000 into $10,000,000.

Chapter 19

What's Changed in Investment Philosophy since the 1990s?

Take Away

There were two major patterns which changed our investment philosophy. First, we identified the flaws in our short-term thinking. Second, was how strong the investment returns were for both the Nifty Fifty as well as the S&P 500 index, which led us to understand better the major impact time and compounding have on our investments.

Verification

Prior to 1990, anyone who did their homework knew that investing for the long term was important. During the 1990's new information changed investment strategies—significantly. There had been for decades the simple formula of:

$$Stock\ Price\ =\ Earnings\ x\ Price\text{-}to\text{-}Earnings\ Ratio$$
$$(Multiple).$$

When looking at past published earnings, or multiple, the numbers are perfect. But, when forecasting future stock prices an investor needs to make two calculations: what the earnings will be and what the multiple will be. If you could know these two numbers for sure your forecast of the price of the stock will be exact.

However, by the end of 1992 a major institutional investment research firm conducted an extensive 10-year study on 1,500 companies to resolve the question of how much of a stock's one-year performance was due to its earnings, versus its multiple. It is important for you to understand this.

The research firm concluded that one-third of a stock's performance for one year was due to earnings and two-thirds was due to its multiple. (Just for the record, our firm recently did its own study and affirmed these numbers). In reality, projecting a stock's earnings one year in advance is subject to change. But earnings estimates are significantly more reliable then the projections of multiples. For individual stocks combining earning and multiple estimates one year out produces a price target no better than an illusion.

To further confuse this subject there were Economists and security analysts who offered their one year projections. The top economists consistently projected a one-year price objective of 8 to 10% higher for the stock market. While, at the same time security analysts were providing a one-year price objective for each stock they recommended. What most investors did with this information was to buy stocks with the expectation of owning them for one to, maybe, three years. During this period a sale would be made and proceeds would be used to repeat the same strategy again and again to achieve their long-term goal. What they were doing was to use short-term thinking to produce long-term returns.

Our firm was one of those who employed this short-term thinking. But in the early 1990s we looked at ourselves in the mirror and said, there's got to be a better way. We began our research with verification. We wanted to know exactly how close earnings and price are related. We did this is 1992.

But we repeat the process for the last five years in the chart that follows for your benefit.

Year	S&P Earnings Change	S&P 500 Price Change
2011	+ 15.12%	0.00%
2012	+ 0.39%	+ 13.41%
2013	+ 10.82%	+ 29.60%
2014	+5.32%	+ 11.39%
2015	- 5.92%	- 0.73%

Just look at these numbers. You don't need to be a financial wizard to figure out how unrelated earnings change and price change are for each year. We knew that we needed to develop an investment philosophy which was genuinely long term.

We began our search by looking backward. We chose to begin our long-term search with the year 1957—the year in which the S&P 500 index was created.

The S&P 500 was new, but it didn't take long for the investment world to accept it as the standard. It simply couldn't be ignored. It represents about 75 percent of the value of all U.S. publicly traded companies. It's a great standard against which to measure your own investment performance. Whether you're a professional or an amateur investor, a mutual fund, a trust department, an insurance company, an independent investment advisor, a broker or a hedge fund manager—comparing your equity returns against the S&P 500 Index is a credible way to know how you're doing.

The S&P Index is not unchanging. What is? Among the 500 stocks in the index, less than five percent may disappear each year due to mergers, acquisitions, stock values dropping below the required $4 billion market capitalization per company. But that makes 95 percent of the paper portfolio passive. Not everyone agreed with this. Because it was a paper portfolio, no one could actually own the index. As a result, some believed it to be an illegitimate comparative. This opinion remained for nearly 20 years.

In the interim, by 1970, the Nifty Fifty Portfolio was constructed. This was a list of what was believed to be fifty of the greatest growth companies in the country. The objective was to buy all fifty stocks and never sell them. It was the first passive portfolio. However, in the early 1970s the Nifty Fifty was peaking in price. In 1973-1974 the stock market went down about 35 percent. While the great Nifty Fifty companies went down over 50 percent (many of these stocks were down 70 percent). The buy and hold forever concept was nearly tarnished to the point of extinction.

That is until 1976, when Vanguard introduced the S&P 500 Index Fund. It was the first fund that investors could actually buy which was designed to replicate the index. Investors weren't sure how closely the fund could mimic the index. Nor were the expense of management well understood. Plus, investors were skeptical of the passive concept—mostly because of the Nifty Fifty. As a result, the reception of the index fund was lukewarm at first, but slowly began to gain acceptance. During all of this, individuals as well as professional investors maintained a short-term investment strategy even though they knew that their goal was long term.

In spite of the negative impressions about the Nifty Fifty in the mid-1990's, Jeremy Siegel, professor at Wharton Business School wrote an article in Barron's Magazine which analyzed how the Nifty Fifty performed from the end of 1972 through 1997, twenty-five years later. There were a number of conclusions which came out of this analysis that were virtually unknown until the Forbes publication. Everyone knew that the Nifty Fifty collapsed in 1973-1974. It was almost universally agreed upon the reason for the collapse was the fact that the stocks in the Nifty Fifty had a price-earnings ratio of 42 in 1972 which compared to a price of the S&P 500 which had a price-earnings ratio of 19: over twice as expensive.

What Jeremy did was to bring up to date what happened had the Nifty Fifty been held for 25 years. It produced an annual rate of return of 11.6% compared to 12.0% for the S&P 500: nearly identical. How was this possible? Starting with a portfolio with a multiple of 42, witnessing a collapse in the first few years and then producing nearly identical investment returns after twenty-five years. The answer is earnings growth. The Nifty Fifty grew earnings 3% per year faster than the S&P 500: 12% versus 9%. Three percent more per year may not sound like much but it is enormous as you will see. In fact, the 3% caused our firm to totally rethink our investment strategy.

The first thing that we did was to reexamine the S&P 500 Index since it was the bell weather for all investors. At the same time, we compared the returns of the index to the returns of the S&P 500 Fund. We were a bit surprised to find out that the returns were virtually identical. If one would step back to the beginnings of the S&P 500 and look at the rate of return for each twenty-five-year period since then (there were 33 such periods), the compounded annual rate of return per period ranged from 8% to 14% with the average being just a touch over 10%.

The chart that follows shows how that 1990-2015 looks. It's an important chart. Memorize it.

S&P 500 Index Price & Price Appreciation Plus Dividend 1990-2015

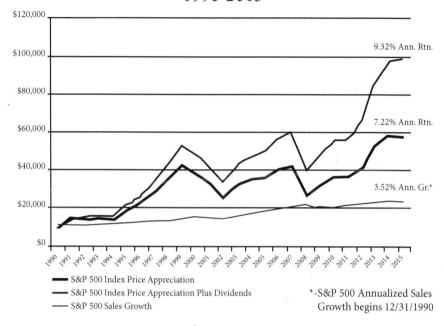

S&P 500 Index Price Appreciation
S&P 500 Index Price Appreciation Plus Dividends
S&P 500 Sales Growth

*-S&P 500 Annualized Sales Growth begins 12/31/1990

Summary

The oxymoron is: the long term is more predictable than the short term. A 10% annual rate of return is well within reach. And as the Nifty Fifty showed, it's possible to identify companies that will grow earnings 3% faster than the S&P 500.

Chapter 20
The Cost of Money Management

Take Away

Before you invest, learn the cost of money management. Although each taxable investor has their own tax bracket, we have calculated that the average investor incurs a cost for money management of about 2 1/2 % per year.

Verification

Even though Wall Street uses indices for comparative purposes, we believe there is a more legitimate alternative. The S&P 500 Index is not available to investors as it is a paper portfolio. However, the S&P500 Index Fund is for real. (During this seminar, whatever is said about the future at the S&P 500 index fund will also apply to the S&P 500 ETF.) It has investors who own the fund and its returns are after the deduction of expenses.

This 10% annual rate of return by the S&P 500 Index fund doesn't mean much until it is compared to the rates of return posted by all the other managers who supervise common stock portfolios. There are all types of investment managers—from mutual funds, to bankers, to insurance companies, to independent advisors, to hedge funds, to brokers, and the list goes on-and-on. The only way to measure the index funds' returns versus the return of the other managers is by using the same criteria for each. The criteria used is pretty straight forward: it is the rate of return for each after accounting for the operating expenses (mostly management fees), trading costs (commissions) and personal taxes. Each of these require a bit of explanation, but before I do so, let me take a moment to remind you of something very important.

That is, make sure to calculate the total expense of investment management BEFORE you invest.

Let's use the mutual fund industry as an example for calculating your total expenses. This is not to pick on mutual funds. Rather, I chose them because their disclosure is far better than trust departments, or insurance companies, or independent managers, or others.

Mutual fund companies really provide a lot of useful information. We're not going to second-guess their marketing information. But we are going to look at their expenses. Basically, a mutual fund has two expenses. The first is called the expense ratio.

This is pretty cut-and-dried and it is well spelled out in the fund's prospectus.

The average large cap mutual fund has an expense ratio of over 1% annually. However, there are many well established funds with a ratio of under 1% per year.

Now, what about trading costs? From a trading cost standpoint, much has changed over the last fifteen years or so. Electronic trading has increased from next-to-nothing to its current status of accounting for over 70% of all activity on the major exchanges. Much of this is due to the fact that the market no longer trades in fractions, now it's in decimals. Between volume and the decimal system, the spread between the bid and ask have been squeezed. This has reduced what's called 'implicit trading costs' as well as commissions they charge.

As a result, trading costs have been reduced significantly and aren't as much of a factor to money managers or clients. Nonetheless, it is a factor, and, it's complicated.

Major large cap funds pay commissions on trades and its addressed in their prospectus B. What's not seen is the implicit costs—most of which is the spread between the bid and ask which becomes a part of the trading costs. However, because of the size and sophistication of these funds, managers can reduce trading costs by electronic trading.

The upshot of all this is that there is no way to accurately assign a trading cost factor. So, I submit the following formula for portfolio trading costs for the major large cap funds. Determine annual turnover (which is easily found in the prospectus) and assume one basis point expense for every 1% of annual turnover. If anything, this should understate trading cost expenses that large cap mutual funds incur. For example, a 30% annual turnover equals 0.3% per year cost. For our calculations, we use 0.3% as our annual trading cost knowing that it could be an understatement.

Finally, we must consider taxes. For the taxable investor, the variance in tax rates can be dramatic. Minimum tax rates for capital gains are 15% while the highest rate can exceed 35%. And income tax rates are subject to wide spreads. At the end of 2012, the federal tax rate for capital gains and dividend income was 15%. In addition, many states and some cities had their own income taxes.

For 2013, all of this changed. For the higher tax-bracketed investor, such as those whose portfolios we managed, tax rates went up significantly. Capital gains and dividend taxes (Cap/Div tax) increased to 20%. In addition, a Medicare net investment tax of 3.8% was added. Federal taxes increased from 15% to 23.8%, an increase of 58.7%. Apart from that, if you live in the likes of Illinois, as I do, where the state income tax rate is 5%, your total cap/div tax rate will be 30%. Even though we have wealthy clients, we reduced this to 25% on the basis that many states don't have income taxes and we didn't want it said that we were overstating taxes to make a point.

Mutual funds producing annual returns will be taxed on dividends of about 2% per year and capital gain distributions of near 5% per year. These two forms of returns equal 7.5% times 30% tax rate for an annual tax of 2.25% per year for those in a higher bracket. We do the same thing for the lowest tax bracket investors. As a result, we have two rather conflicting cost pictures.

	Higher Tax Bracket Clients	Lower Tax Bracket Clients
Expense Ratio	.75%	0.75%
Trading Costs	.30%	0.30%
Taxes	2.25%	1.12%
Total	3.30%	2.17%

We use 2.5% as a guideline for investors. Is it correct? No. Each individual has their own tax rate. Nevertheless, it's a good guideline. Keep in mind that over time, these rates can and will change: so stay alert.

For our calculations, we will assume 2.5% for annual expenses. So, the question is how much do expenses affect investment returns?

Let's begin with the S&P 500 Index Fund growing at 10% per year. For our Index fund, we use the Vanguard S&P 500 Index Fund as our comparative. It was the original and is currently the largest of such funds.

This fund has a management fee of .05% per year. Because there's so little turnover in a passive portfolio, trading costs are virtually nonexistent. There haven't been any capital gain distributions from the fund in more than a decade. This leaves dividends, which have run at a touch over 2% per year.

Using our 25% dividend income tax rate (or .5%) our gross returns will go down from 10% to 9.5%. And over twenty-five years, our $1,000,000 will have increased to $10,650,000. If we go though the same arithmetic with major mutual funds the rate of return will decrease to 7.5% and our $1,000,000 will grow to $6,098,000. That's only 60% of what the passive portfolio would produce. This is a powerful statement that you should understand.

No manager will tell you this—that's not their job. Moreover, in most cases they couldn't even if they wanted to because they don't know what your tax bracket is. What your manager will tell you is what your pretax returns are. It's up to you to pay your taxes.

To put this in perspective, consider the boxes below. This little table tells it all; starting with $1,000,000.

	Pre-tax Returns	After-tax Return
S&P 500 Index Fund	$12,059,000	$10,651,000
Large Cap Fund	$8,180,000	$6,098,000

Remember this: The name of the game is after-tax returns.

This is your money. Make sure you understand the costs of money management. This applies to any investment manager. Your comparative should be the S&P500 Index fund. It is the standard for the industry. Let me help you out a little bit. Did you know that over most any extended period at least 85% of all major stock funds either close their doors or underperform the S&P 500? And that's pre-tax returns. After taxes, hardy anyone does as well as the S&P 500. And the longer you stretch out the holding period the less likely you'll do as well as the market. The headwinds of expenses and taxes are too high to overcome.

The difference between passive and active management is obvious. Passive management is accompanied by very low fees, almost no sales and therefore minimal taxes. Active management is the opposite. This is why our firm recommends that investors have a large percent of their equities invested passively a la the S&P 500 Index Fund.

Back to the mid-1990s. We learned from the Nifty Fifty that it was possible to identify fifty companies whose earnings growth would exceed that of the market by a meaningful amount: 11% versus 8% per year for twenty-five years. This was a major breakthrough.

Then, in 1994 the New Nifty Fifty was constructed by Morgan Stanley. Like its predecessor, it was designed to own great companies with the purpose of never selling anything. We kept tract of this portfolio because we believed in the passive concept. today the portfolio is twenty-one years old. Attached is the portfolio and pre-tax performance of the New Nifty Fifty:

New Nifty Fifty

Ticker	Amount Invested	Growth of $10K	
PM	$10,000.00	$241,938.55	
MSFT	$10,000.00	$207,730.76	
ORCL	$10,000.00	$179,790.18	
BDX	$10,000.00	$175,246.18	
CSCO	$10,000.00	$157,068.46	
TXN	$10,000.00	$150,535.81	
MDT	$10,000.00	$141,709.48	
BestFoods	$10,000.00	$130,583.91	<--Acquired by Unilever in 2000
MCD	$10,000.00	$122,648.35	
INTC	$10,000.00	$121,250.93	
JNJ	$10,000.00	$120,356.24	
ADP	$10,000.00	$107,080.01	
AXP	$10,000.00	$106,286.97	
BMY	$10,000.00	$105,411.38	
Mobil	$10,000.00	$101,882.29	<--Merged November 30, 1999
ABT	$10,000.00	$100,386.93	
IBM	$10,000.00	$98,735.52	
MMM	$10,000.00	$98,244.25	
AHP	$10,000.00	$96,006.99	<--Ticker changed to WYE on 3/11/2002,
LLY	$10,000.00	$95,609.02	then purchased by Pfizer on 10/16/2009
PEP	$10,000.00	$92,204.29	
BA	$10,000.00	$91,504.73	
PFE	$10,000.00	$90,564.39	
GIS	$10,000.00	$90,236.61	
Exxon	$10,000.00	$87,730.03	<--Merged November 30, 1999
DIS	$10,000.00	$86,368.26	
PG	$10,000.00	$83,743.11	
SGP	$10,000.00	$82,436.69	<--Acquired by Merck on 11/4/2009
HNZ	$10,000.00	$80,329.03	<--Acquired by Berkshire on 6/10/2013
BEAM	$10,000.00	$76,819.44	<--Acquired by Suntory Holdings on 5/1/2014
Gillette	$10,000.00	$72,852.56	<--Bought by Proctor&Gamble 10/3/2005
SLE	$10,000.00	$72,566.43	<--Acquired by TSN on 8/29/2014
GE	$10,000.00	$65,442.12	
MRK	$10,000.00	$57,254.76	
CAG	$10,000.00	$54,328.19	
KO	$10,000.00	$52,710.73	
DD	$10,000.00	$49,039.02	
K	$10,000.00	$44,858.63	
CPB	$10,000.00	$42,611.89	
T	$10,000.00	$42,260.65	
HPQ	$10,000.00	$35,460.68	
AMP	$10,000.00	$30,985.20	<--Acquired by Tyco on 4/5/1999
LYX	$10,000.00	$27,026.23	<--Acquired by BP on 4/18/2000
BAC	$10,000.00	$26,768.67	
C	$10,000.00	$14,666.69	
MSI	$10,000.00	$12,265.14	
XRX	$10,000.00	$8,818.31	
EK	$10,000.00	$8.93	
ENE	$10,000.00	$-	
	$490,000.00	$4,230,363.65	

			CAGR
Total Return*		763.34%	10.81%
S&P 500*		550.81%	9.33%
Dow Jones*		618.93%	9.85%

Securities we did not price due to corporate events
EDS <--Acquired by GM in 1984, later spunoff in 1996, then bought by HPQ in 8/26/2008
Source: Bloomberg

Unlike the original Nifty Fifty that had a beginning price earnings ratio twice as high as the S&P 500, the New Nifty Fifty and the S&P 500 started with very close multiples. As a result, there was a notable difference between investment returns. The New Nifty Fifty compounded at 10.8% per year versus the S&P 500 at 9.3%. We've been following the portfolio and return comparisons for its lifetime, twenty- one years. $1,000,000 invested in the New Nifty Fifty grew to $8,616,000 while the S&P 500 grew to $6,472,000. That's pre-tax, not after tax.

Neither the New Nifty Fifty nor the S&P had hardly any operating costs because they each were passive portfolios. But what it does demonstrate is that a carefully constructed portfolio, held for a long time, can beat the market. And that's what our firm was out to do.

Summary

Understand the difference between active management and passive management and learn the expenses of money management before you invest. Active management can cost about 2 ½ % more per year versus passive management. As Jack Bogle, the founder of Vanguard and the S&P 500 has said, "You get what you don't pay for."

Chapter 21
The Smythe Portfolio

Take Away

With all of these changes in investment philosophy in mind, our firm began to develop our own passive portfolio for our taxable clients. The difference between what we were doing and what our competitors were doing was that our goal was to raise after-tax returns—something our competition barely considered, if at all.

Verification

By the end of 2002, we had published a guideline portfolio for all taxable clients. The purpose of the portfolio was to have it incorporated into a client's overall portfolio to the most logical extent possible. Frequently, the clients already owned some very suitable stocks at a low-cost basis which shouldn't be touched.

There were similarities and differences between existing passive portfolios and our own passive portfolios. What was most similar was the expected time frame for the investment decision: 25 years. By design, our selection criteria were different. We never intended to have a totally passive portfolio. In fact, it was intended that the portfolio would be about 90% passive and 10% active. What we knew was that no matter how carefully a portfolio was put together, a la the New Nifty Fifty, over time some of the stocks should have been sold. If, over time, the bottom 20% of the stocks are a drag on performance, they should be sold. Our intention was to retain our greatest strength, the sell decision (which we will cover later). We knew that had the Nifty Fifty portfolios been able to sell their losers, they could have enhanced their returns. Some active management would more than take care of that. We also wished to retain the sell decision as it related to harvesting losses. (again, to be covered later).

By providing for harvesting it eliminates a disadvantage that purely passive portfolios have. That would include the likes of index funds. A purely passive portfolio cannot sell individual stocks... therefore, no harvesting.

In 2002, our firm formally introduced our own near passive portfolio. To a great extent, we approached the building of the portfolio on the same basis as the two Nifty Fifties pursued. In particular, our selection process for individual stocks focused on top quality proprietary growth companies. In this regard, we were almost identical. However, there were some differences in how we handled the portfolio once it was selected.

Before we get into these differences, I think it's helpful to revisit the New Nifty Fifty and analyze how the top ten stocks performed over the last twenty-one years, versus how the bottom ten stocks performed.

At inception, $10,000 was invested in each stock. Below is what each of these stocks are now worth.

The 10 Best			The 10 Worst	
Philip Morris	241,938		Campbells	42,611
Microsoft	207,730		American Tel	42,280
Oracle	179,790		Hewlett Packard	36,460
Becton	175,246		AMP	30,985
Cisco	157,068		LYX	27,062
Texas Inst.	150,535		Bank America	26,768
Medtronics	141,709		Motorola	12,265
Bestfoods	130,583		XRX	8,818
McDonald's	122,648		Eastman Kodak	9
Intel	121,250		Enron	0

The bottom line is that the top ten, or top 20%, of the New Nifty Fifty produced $1,500,000 of the total value of the portfolio of $4,100,000. That represents 37% of the ending value. Meanwhile, the bottom ten, also 20% of the New Nifty Fifty was reduced to 2% of the portfolio value.

We believe that any passive portfolio will produce a similar pattern whereby a limited percent of stocks within that portfolio will account for a disproportionate percent of the gains while at the other end a limited number of stocks will be a real drag on overall performance.

Consensus opinion would claim that 50 stocks is under-diversification, while we believe the opposite. Conventional wisdom says diversify, diversify, diversify, and volatility is reduced. That is true to a minor degree when you are talking about a stock portfolio. But the question is, is this the full story? I, for one, don't believe it. There is another way to control volatility—it's called quality.

The firm has always been of the opinion that diversification is a two-edged sword. Just a casual look at the S&P 500 helps this point. The S&P 500 has a total market value equal to about 75% of all publicly traded U.S. corporations.

By comparison, the Dow Jones Industrial averages are comprised of 30 companies. What's interesting is the fact that these 30 companies are also in the S&P 500, but represent only 6% of all the stocks in the S&P 500. However, they represent just over 30% of the market value of the S&P Index. Obviously, the market cap of the average Dow stock is significantly higher than that of the average S&P stock. This is important when you consider the following...

From a rate of return standpoint, the two indices have produced very similar investment returns. For several years at a time, one will outperform the other only to reverse themselves for the next period of years. But, for the most part, these swings in performance tend to offset each other thereby producing nearly identical returns. From a total return standpoint, the last twenty-five years are a good example (1990-2015). The S&P 500 compounded at 9.3% while the DOW was 9.8%. But, over the past 50 years, the S&P has slightly out-produced the DOW. From our standpoint, not only has the rate of return been equal, so has volatility been equal. In other words, quality offsets diversification.

So how did our firm go about selecting companies for our own Smythe Portfolio, you might ask? Well, we knew that we were after companies that were going to be around for a long time, companies with economic moat. So we started by compiling a list of large-cap companies. Yes, there are many good smaller companies, but we're looking for as much predictability as we can find.

Ideal criteria include:
- a proprietary product
- market dominance
- pricing power

For our purposes, value stocks aren't very appealing. They'll be around for a long time, but they're not likely to grow much.

What about cyclical or commodity stocks? Cyclical stocks, as their name suggests, go up and down with the general economy. Commodity stocks are nearly the same. Each require counter-intuition. The best returns will be achieved by buying the stock at the low point of its earnings—which coincides with a high price-earnings ratio—and selling the stock during the opposite scenario. But, can anyone accurately anticipate a recession? Economists have been trying to do that forever, without much success. When will the next recession arrive? How long will it last? How severe will it be? And if we were to buy cyclicals, we may have to sell them in only a few years, depending on the economy's ups and downs. Both are too dangerous and don't fit well into our permanent vision.

Our firm, on the other hand, has a natural bias toward growth companies.

Beyond those characteristics of every great company, we look first and foremost at revenue growth and free cash flow. Basically, it's a tradeoff between those two factors.

Companies with the highest revenue growth may reinvest all their earnings, leaving no free cash flow. Those with lower revenue growth may have free cash flow which can be used for such things as dividends, acquisitions and share repurchases. Although our preference is revenue growth, we often invest in companies that have both revenue growth and free cash flow.

What may surprise you is the price we're willing to pay for those great companies. We look for stocks that are selling at a price-earnings ratio that is 25-50 percent higher than the average price-earnings ratio for the market.

Crazy? Not when you have a 25-year vision.

If you go to a jeweler, and ask to see the range of one-carat diamonds available, the jeweler may show you stones ranging in price from $1,000 to $10,000. You go into an auto showroom and ask to see all the models of the brand you're interested in. They may range in price from $25,000 to $100,000.

Are you getting more for your money when you buy the expensive diamond, or the expensive car? Usually you are, and in the world of investment it's the same thing: Higher quality and growth means higher price. Premium quality equates with premium pricing.

The collective knowledge of the markets and the billions and billions of dollars invested in them pretty much determines the price of every asset in the market. The collective knowledge knows what high quality is. But the real question is, how many high-quality companies are great investments? That's more difficult to answer.

Let me put this in perspective for you. The Dow Jones averages has 30 high quality companies. However, only 6 of these stocks fit our criteria. If we look at this from the S&P 500 standpoint, there's fewer than 100 stocks to be considered by us. And once you consider revenue growth and cash flows, the list dwindles down to about 20 stocks at any one time. If we can determine that the revenue growth and cash flow are sustainable, we will pay a premium for them and hopefully keep them until death when we part.

Summary

So, what we learned at this point was to balance our passive portfolio (i.e. S&P 500 fund) with a mix of select individual stocks that mirror our Smythe Portfolio approach.

Chapter 22

The Sell Decision

Take Away

To maximize your returns, buy stocks with an intent to own them forever. That said, there will be times when it is wise to sell a particular stock. When deciding when and what to sell, it's impossible to do it based upon market timing. We'll show you when and why to sell.

Verification

Secondly, when selecting companies, think long-term. We look for two factors: Proprietary companies with high revenue growth.

Ask money managers which investment decision is the most difficult for them to make and they will most likely respond, "The decision of when to sell."

Wall Street simply isn't set up to make sell decisions. In fact, for all practical purposes, Wall Street doesn't make sell decisions.

It all basically starts with the security analysts who may specialize his research efforts on a group of stocks like energy, or health care, etc.

The analyst is competing in an information war with other analysts who research the same group of stocks. They may be twenty or forty top-notch analysts involved with covering the same stock or stocks. They're all pros and, as a result, will review the same information in a similar way. Collectively, these analysts will provide recommendations ranging from: strong buy, buy, hold, etc. But, as you look at the number of analysts who agree with each other, it is surprising how the large majority of recommendations overlap.

For example, let's look at the recommendation made for our three stocks: AMZN, IBM and PM

Analyst Recommendation	AMZN	IBM	PM
Buy	29	6	8
Overweight	5	2	2
Hold	11	19	6
Underweight	0	1	0
Sell	0	1	1

This is typical: almost no underweights or sells.

In other words, you're on your own as to when to sell. Let me provide you with a little background information before we try to tackle the when to sell issue.

When asked, investors tend to believe that the market is up half the time and down the other half. Not so. Between 1954 and 2015, the market was up 48 years and down 13 years. That's about 75% of the years that the market is up. This is not only a strong endorsement for the permanent vision, it points out how difficult it is to predict when the market will, or has, peaked. Take 2013, for example.

Each of the preceding four years, the market was up. Does this mean that the next year, 2013, was likely to be a down year? Consider this:

Each year the most recognized pundits of Wall Street make a prediction as to where the market will be twelve months hence. For 2013, the forecast was again a 9% gain. Does this imply that if the market should be sold if it goes higher than 9% by any meaningful amount? As it turned out, total return for the market for that year was 32%. Had you sold the market at any time prior to year-end, you would have been premature since the market hit an all-time high on the last day of the year. And, not to be forgotten, the pundits' collective opinion for what the market will do in the next twelve months is always around 9%. In essence, they're giving a long-term projection (a permanent vision) for a short-term question. They know no better. No one does.

Some will call for a decline in the market of, say 20%. But, that's a hard call to make or to justify. Below is a list of all the years since 1957 that the market declined 20% or more in one year and a listing of all the years the market increased 20% or more in one calendar year:

Down at least 20%, in one year		Up at least 20%, in one year	
Year	**Percent Down**	**Year**	**Percent Up**
1974	-26%	1958	+43%
2002	-22%	1961	+26%
2008	-37%	1975	+37%
		1980	+32%
		1985	+32%
		1989	+32%
		1994	+31%
		1995	+37%
		1996	+23%
		1997	+33%
		1998	+28%
		1999	+21%
		2009	+26%
		2013	+32%

Knowing all of this, we believe it's nearly impossible to predict the top of a market. As a result, we remain fully invested all the time. For us, the market timing decision is out. The permanent vision decision is in. There are several forms of the sell decision beyond making the wholesale decision to sell everything. We employ two types of sell decisions. However, our strategies are stock specific as opposed to market timing in nature.

Harvesting losses is one of our primary strategies. It is used almost exclusively in bear markets as it is more a tax decision than it is an investment decision. It works like this. Assume the stock market is down 20%. Chances are you will have stocks which have declined by a similar percent. And, it's very probable that some of your stocks are now in a loss position, particularly if they were recent purchases.

Let's assume we have a group of stocks which are down at least 20%. We may make the tax decision to sell some, or all of these stocks for the sole purpose of establishing losses. These losses are worth something. They can offset established gains or be used to offset future gains, thereby reducing taxes and increasing rates of return.

Once the sale has been made, we have two choices for the money. We can buy a very similar group of stocks or repurchase the same stocks in 31 days, which will avoid the wash sale rule. Either way, we don't basically alter the portfolio. And, we don't count it as turnover, even though technically it is, because it's a tax decision—not an investment decision.

We have found that the best time to harvest losses is when the stock market itself has declined and dragged our stocks down with it.

If we can assure ourselves that the stock is going down because of negative external news, like the housing/financial debacle, we will harvest by selling our losing stocks.

In order to identify stocks which should be sold, we use what's called relative strength to help identify those companies. That is the relationship between the S&P 500 Index and each individual stock traded. It works like this. It indicated how each stock is performing relative to the S&P 500 over the last two-hundred days. On a scale of 1 to 100, the average stock has a relative strength of 50—the same as the S&P 500. Any stock that is declining less than the S&P is performing better than the S&P, and anything below 50 is under-performing.

We are looking to sell our under-performers. However, when we have the opposite situation—when the market is going up or doing nothing and a stock we own is down, say 20%—we will likely sell. We know from experience that this type of relative strength is usually a precursor to negative news. Most likely, we will not buy the stock back, nor will we buy a look-alike stock to replace it. Instead, we'll go elsewhere.

Obviously, we support our decision with fundamental research. Analysts' opinions don't help much because collectively they are nearly always of the opinion that 50% of all stocks are buys, 45% holds and 5% sells.

This is not to say that Wall Street doesn't provide negative information. They do; but by default, it's up to you (or your advisor)—the investor—to determine whether or not you should convert this information into a sell decision. That's why the sell decision is considered the hardest investment decision to make.

It is right in this area that we believe our greatest strength lays. As an asset manager, it's in our DNA to look for negative fundamental change and when we do, we sell the stock. Most often this happens when the wind has changed from at our backs to in our face.

Most investors think about selling a stock differently than we do. Their emphasis is on at what price does a stock become over-priced, prompting a sale on the premise that you'll never go broke taking a profit. That's baloney. The more accurate premise is that you'll never have satisfactory returns if you sell your great stocks and keep your mediocre stocks. One of the most expensive errors an investor makes is when they sell a stock after it doubles and then it continues to go up another three or four-fold, thereby carrying the portfolio. Had you sold many of these stocks, investment performance would have been dismal.

Selling great companies who have endurance contradicts the permanent vision concept. We never sell just because we think a stock is overpriced because no one seems to know what that price is. We do sell when the fundamentals of a company turn negative. However, in practice, great companies seldom turn decisively negative. Those that had a material negative change were generally caused by competition which displaced the product of our company. Technology companies are vulnerable to negative change.

This is not to imply that quality companies can't fail. Eastman Kodak was a premier company for decades and for all practical purposes, it's gone. What the quality statement does say is, when compared to mid-cap and small-cap stocks, these large-cap companies have staying power and are much less likely to fail than are the smaller companies. Fewer failure equals higher returns and—as Monsieur St. Luc might say—quality will endure.

Summary

Before we go any further, let's recap some of the things which have been discussed: Short-term thinking is significantly more speculative than long-term compounding.

Our firm learned endurance from the St. Luc Family. And the thought process was embellished by the S&P 500 and the two Nifty Fifties. As a result, the long- term thinking process is at the heart of our investment philosophy.

What we added to this was the 'quality will prevail' thesis, which produced our permanent vision. Plus, the compounding at 10% was supported by history. We supplied the two primary factors of revenue and cash flow, which helped identify the differences between a great company and a great investment. We also supplied the analysis of expenses and taxes, as well as how they reduced investment returns. And, we advocated two forms of sales: harvesting losses and outright sales.

Chapter 23

Loss Aversion and the Legendary Lugano Poker Game

Take Away

By nature, humans are risk averse and hate to lose or make a mistake. But there's a difference between poker and investing – a huge difference.

Verification

This is as good a time as any for us to imagine, for a few minutes, that we are not here but in a huge casino in Lugano playing poker at the five-card stud table. We're watching a legendary game, one for the history books.

There are 10 players. You are one of the them.

But first—let's look at another table—one you must understand in order to truly comprehend the stakes in this game. The chart shows you the probability of getting a truly history-making hand in this game we're about to observe. You'll notice that one pair or no pairs account for more than 92 percent of all hands. It shows the probability of various hands, using five cards from a 52-card deck.

Type of Hand	Number	Odds: 1 Chance In…	Percentage of All Hands
Straight Flush	40	64,974	0.0015
Four of a Kind	624	4,165	0.024
Full House	3,744	694	0.144
Flush	5,108	509	0.197
Straight	10,200	255	0.392
Three of a Kind	54,912	47	2.11
Two Pair	123,552	21	4.75
One Pair	1,098,240	2.4	42.26
No Pair	1,302,540	2.0	50.12
All Hands: Total	2,598,960		100

So—the game begins with everyone, including you, putting in an anti of $100. Each player is dealt one card down and one card up.

The betting begins with you because you have a queen, the highest card showing.

You know that a pair of queens doesn't often win. Particularly if there are as many as 10 players.

You bet the pot limit of $1,000 in hopes of driving out the other players. Three people call your bet.

There is now $5,000 in the pot.

The next card is turned. Your queen is still the best card. You bet $5,000. Only one player (let's call him C) calls.

The pot is now worth $15,000.

The next card doesn't improve either hand, so you bet the maximum $15,000. Player C calls.

The pot is now $45,000.

Why would C stay in the hand? We see his six, eight, and jack of clubs showing.

What down card could he have that would make him a threat? It could be a pair. But even if he does have a pair, the chances of catching a six, eight, or jack are not very good.

Also, the three cards showing are all clubs, so it's likely that his down card is also a club, and that all he needs is to draw another club to win. But, again, the odds are not very good. He has to beat the odds in order to win the hand.

The next card you are dealt does nothing for your hand. Player C is dealt the king of hearts, which makes his, the high hand showing. He has to bet or check (do nothing). He bets $45,000. This is a giant bet. Everyone grows still.

You are stunned that he bet at all. You're almost breathless at the $45,000 bet. You believed—and still believe—he's drawing for a flush. You never considered that his face-down card could be the king of clubs, which would give him a pair of kings, bettering your pair of queens.

You analyze, as you sit there, the history of Player C's hand.

When he had three cards, he called a $5,000 bet to see the next card. A dumb call. Then he paid $15,000 to see the next card. Why? You're sure that he knows the odds of drawing two clubs in a row are about 1-in-35. His odds of catching a fourth club of any kind are about one-in-four—not very good odds.

At this point in the game you are quite certain that he has four clubs. But, maybe he had a kicker, the king of clubs. Maybe that's why he bet the $45,000.

Or maybe it's all a bluff.

Maybe he didn't have to have the king clubs. Maybe all he needed to do was to draw any king or ace. If he drew the king or ace of clubs, surely he would have his flush. If he drew the king or ace in any other suit, surely he could hold the club companion, which would beat the pair of queens.

What to do?

Call or fold?

What if you call, and he does have the king of clubs? What if you fold and he doesn't have the king of clubs? If you call, and he doesn't have the second king, you're a hero. If you fold, at least you won't lose $45,000.

What to do?

Calling a large final bet is the most dangerous part of a poker game. Such big bets are usually genuine. Players who make a practice of calling such bets, however, usually lose.

You still have to choose, and the clock is ticking. Ticking, ticking, ticking...

The five-card poker game we've just participated in—and investing in Wall Street—are not the same thing. But some of the issues are the same: you, the player, don't want to lose. You really, really, really, don't want to lose. You don't want to do the wrong thing.

Clinical psychologists, in interviewing players of games of all kinds, have found that fear of losing carries an emotional punch double that of winning. Winning is great, but fear of losing is overwhelmingly awful.

What does such a poker game have to do with investing?

The poker game is 100% risk versus reward. In the investment world of portfolio management, it is price volatility versus reward. You can lose all your money in a single stock. But you can't lose all of your portfolio. In fact, the stock market has

had repeated declines. Some as great as a 50% decline. But always, always, always the stock market has recovered and, in time, made new highs.

So, let's get this straight. It is not the stock market that will lose you money. Rather, it is your behavior which will lose you money. More than anything else, how you react to the fear of loss will determine whether you will win or lose.

Summary

It is essential that you learn how to control fear of loss. It is not the stock market that will lose you money. Rather, it is your behavior which will lose you money. More than anything else, how you react to the fear of loss will determine whether you win or lose.

Chapter 24

Dealing with Volatility

Take Away

How you handle a significant decline in the market may be the single most important investment decision you'll make in a lifetime? You need to plan today for how you will deal with a decline, that is inevitable to occur.

Verification

In market terms, volatility means that the market may go down any percent. But, it will ultimately recover and make new highs. The market has been true to this definition since it has always recovered to new highs. The recent 50% decline in 2008-2009 was followed by new highs in late 2013-2014. There were only two other occasions in the last 100 years that the market declined 50%. It's a seldom occasion.

It is basically a given that the market will decline 25% sometime in the next 25 years—our investment time horizon. So, the question becomes, can you stomach a 25% decline in an equity portfolio or will you capitulate to fear and sell? Think about this as though you are retired, you had a portfolio just large enough to support your standard of living—which now looks unlikely—and the only hope you have is a permanent vision which now looks like an illusion.

As best you can, you need to identify how much volatility you can stand. One way to alter volatility is through the use of asset allocation—that is the percentage of your portfolio invested in stocks versus bonds.

There is a methodology which can help you determine the degree of volatility that you can endure. It's called the asset allocation decision. Basically, this decision is the percentage of your investments which you would like in stocks as well as bonds.

But, before we go into this let's talk about bonds. This is the only time we're going to speak of bonds because in our opinion, for the taxable investor, bonds are a terrible investment.

For the past half-century, the S&P 500 index fund has produced an annual after-tax return of 9.5%. For the past half-century, the average ten-year bond has produced a pre- tax yield of near 5%. And once taxes of 25% are considered, that yield is reduced to 3.75%.

% invested in stocks	% invested in bonds	% decline of portfolio
100%	0%	-25%
75%	25%	-18.75%
50%	50%	-12.5%
25%	75%	-6.25%
0%	100%	-0%

Some would contend that the historical 3% rate of inflation should be deducted from these returns. If so, stock returns are reduced to 6.5% while bonds are reduced to 0.75% per year.

Any way you want to look at it, compared to stocks, bonds are a horrible investment. So, why would any taxable entity or person invest in bonds? In our opinion, there's only two answers: to reduce inevitable portfolio price volatility, or to have a short-term fund available for living expenses or emergencies.

Allocation can reduce volatility as demonstrated below; this assumes that stocks will go down 25% while bonds remain unchanged in price.

Let's assume that you make the determination that you won't be able to sleep at night if your portfolio were to decline by more than 12.5%. In other words, your asset allocation is a comforting 50% stocks and 50% bonds.

Unfortunately, there's a second chart. This chart won't let you sleep with a 50/50 allocation. It looks at the same subject from a different direction. This chart shows how much a change in allocation will affect 25-year returns assuming 10% compounding for stocks and a historical yield, for bonds, of 5%. (Remember, this is before expenses and taxes.)

% of portfolio invested in stocks @ 10%	% of portfolio invested in bonds @ 5%	Combined return	$1,000,000 dollar amount in 25 years
100% @ 10%	0	10%	$10,835,000
75% @ 10%	25% @ 5%	8.75%	$8,142,000
50% @ 10%	50% @ 5%	7.5%	$6,098,000
25% @ 10%	75% @ 5%	6.25%	$4,552,000
0	100% @ 5%	5%	$3,886,000

Again, it has been often said that the asset allocation decision is the single most important investment decision that you'll ever make. So, look hard at the two tables.

It will take you no time to figure out that the allocation decision is a catch 22. The more you reduce volatility, the more you reduce your returns and visa-versa.

Often an investor will determine how much return they need from their investments and they go to the second table first to see what asset allocation will deliver their desired returns. Then they go back to the volatility table to see what the volatility will be for that allocation. It may well be beyond what they can stand. This leaves some hard choices.

They either cut spending or stay employed or change their behavior. The specific behavior that has to be changed is the fear factor. Not fear itself, but how you react to fear. Selling your portfolio because you capitulated to fear is, in my opinion, the worst conceivable decision you could possibly make. So, what does one need to do to guarantee that they won't capitulate to fear? They need behavioral conviction.

If you don't mind, let's make a detour back to Lugano where you're looking at a genuine $45,000 bet or a bluff. Like it or not, you are faced with loss aversion which breeds fear. There's no way to know for sure what you should do. What is certain is that if you do call the bet and it's no bluff, you will lose all of the money you already put in the pot plus $45,000. That's a loss of 100%--no wonder loss aversion accompanies such a bet.

But there's a difference in the loss aversion of a poker hand and the loss aversion present in the stock market. As the stock market goes down, down, down, fear goes up, up, up. Take for example a $1,000,000 portfolio that the investor has in stocks with the goal of living off the income and capital appreciation which is expected with a permanent vision. The market begins to decline an ordinary amount, say 15%. And then the news gets more bearish and prices begin to accelerate on the downside and the market is down 25%... and the news and prices are getting worse by the day and before you know it, your portfolio is down 30% and you face panic. Suddenly you recognize that your portfolio is down $300,000 and what you have left won't support you. And, if you think you would face loss aversion when you lose a $45,000 poker bet, wait until your portfolio declines $300,000.

Does that mean that I'm a pessimist? Absolutely not, but, I virtually guarantee you that sometime during this quarter century the stock market will decline at least 25%. What you can't do is try and figure out what to do when it happens. Rather you need to prepare yourself well in advance—like now.

There are two components of this preparation: Probabilities and Behavior. The probability of a decline of at least 25% being followed by all-time highs in the market is 100%. Or, at least that's historically so. If that's true, why does a market decline create such fear, which in turn produces capitulation?

It's pretty simple to figure out why behavior overcomes probabilities for the retiree. His or her equity portfolio just went down 30% and their permanent vision becomes an illusion, probabilities are meaningless and they're going broke. That may sound too simple of a response, but it's pretty well supported by a couple of indicators. Mutual fund purchases versus liquidation: when mutual funds are being wholesale liquidated it is almost always when fear is rising. This is reinforced by Vix, which measures sentiment within the marketplace. It's like a thermometer: the reading goes up as the temperature (fear) rises.

You might keep in mind that if you do the same thing as everyone else you're going to get the same result. And, if there's one specific time when you should not follow the crowd, it's when the crowd is panicked.

Before we move on let me ask you some questions. Do you intend to manage your own investments? If so, ask yourself (or ask your friends) can you admit when you're wrong? And then ask yourself, have you understood what's been said so far in this seminar? If you've said no to either of the last two questions, then, please don't be a part of the management of your own assets.

But if you determine that you should be even a part manager then you should stop and evaluate how you will react to panic. Stop and think. This is one of the most critical periods that you will ever experience in your investment lifetime. It is in that time that you cannot—absolutely cannot—despair.

Think again and again. 2008 was only the third calendar year in the last century that the market has declined over 30%. Think: every market that has declined any percentage has recovered and gone to new highs. Think: every market that goes down is accompanied by fear. Think: a market that has collapsed to this degree does so, because it is accompanied by despair causing investors to liquidate their holdings. Instead, it should ignite a light in your brain that says "opportunity." Fear creates opportunity. How you react during a severe decline in the market may be the single most important investment decision you'll make in a lifetime.

The behavioral goal of the long-term investor is to believe that any decline will be followed by higher highs. If you can truly say it and really believe it, market declines are no longer a risk factor, they are an opportunity factor. Memorize it: *market declines are an opportunity factor*. Once you have converted fear to an opportunity factor you have won the behavior war.

In order to think ahead to the day when you'll need to turn belief in the execution of "fear creates opportunity" requires some advanced training.

The problem is, as said before, that on a one-year basis the price of a stock is about one-third related to the fundamentals (earnings) of a stock, while two- thirds of the price movement is related to market behavior, which shows up in the price-earnings ratio.

One only needs to look back to the market decline of 2008 as well as the market advance in 2013. In the 2008-2009 timeframe, Gross Domestic Product (GDP) declined 4% while corporate earnings declined 29%. Yet the market went down 50%. In 2013, GDP went up 2% while earnings went up 6%. However, in that same year the market had a total return of 32%. It is true that the market is a forecasting machine. But, it is also true that the market over forecasts. It is primarily a function of investors' behavior which ranges from despair to exuberance and back again… and again, and again.

Summary

In order to be a great investor, one needs to know how to play the behavioral game as well as the probability game. These investors recognize that ***behavior rules the near term and probability rules the long term*** and your behavior is more important than any investment equation. Marked declines are an opportunity factor. DON'T EVER PANIC!

Chapter 25

Investment Returns on the Smythe Portfolio

Take Away

We invest in great proprietary companies and hold them as long as possible to avoid expenses and taxes. We invest primarily in companies with strong revenue growth and free cash flow, and we are always looking for negative change.

Verification

We've established the fact that the S&P 500 index fund is the standard for successful long- term investment returns. We've also established the fact that the original Nifty Fifty and the New Nifty Fifty identified companies whose revenues and earnings grew faster than the S&P 500. But, when our firm began constructing the Smythe Portfolio we intentionally modified the passive concept, what we didn't modify was the basic long-term philosophy.

We began our process with the creed, "quality will prevail." We only bought proprietary companies with anticipated sustainable above average revenue and earnings growth and who had large market capitalizations. We believe that these factors produce quality for our portfolio of stocks which is higher quality than 80% of all the stocks that are in the S&P 500.

We were also influenced by the two Nifty Fifties. In each case, they owned large- cap growth stocks. And in each case their earnings growth exceeded that of the S&P 500. What's surprising is how a portfolio of fifty supposedly great stocks produces superior returns. It all boils down to a few stocks. Take for example the New Nifty Fifty. The top ten stocks produce 57% of the portfolio's returns, while the remaining forty stocks produce 43% of the gains.

And this is due to the ten- to-fifteen very poor performance stocks.

The portfolio would have done much better had the worst stocks been sold. Knowing this, we made some adjustments when designing the Smythe Portfolio.

At any point in time we believe that there are at least 100 great large cap companies. But we don't believe that at any point in time that there are more than 25 great companies that are great investments. That's the reason that when we started the Smythe Portfolio we committed to a portfolio of a maximum of twenty-five stocks.

We set an average turnover ratio of 10%. It was intentionally higher than the S&P 500 turnover to allow us the advantage of what we believe to be one of our strongest abilities: the sell decisions—both outright sales and harvesting of loss sales. This is a great advantage over the S&P 500, which basically doesn't do either form of sales. We practice the "keep your winners and sell your losers" ideology.

The S&P 500 fulfils certain goals which the Smythe Portfolio cannot achieve.

And it is also true that the Smythe Portfolio can attain certain goals that the S&P 500 cannot achieve. For example, the S&P has an abundance of diversification—that is, the various sectors of the economy are well covered. The trading of stocks in the open market constantly reshapes the value of each stock and sector. The S&P has a low turnover ratio and, therefore, no capital gains distributions are made, therefore, no capital gains taxes.

On the other hand, the Smythe Portfolio is designed to complement the S&P 500 by concentrating its portfolio holding on stocks that are great companies that are expected to be great investments.

While the average stocks in the S&P 500 has a revenue growth rate of near 2% and an earnings growth rate of 6%, the top ten stocks of the Smythe Portfolio is concentrated in companies, who for the next three-to-five years should increase revenue by 14% per year and earning by 18%... and then decelerate. The table that follows shows the results of the ten largest stocks in the Smythe Portfolio:

Stocks	Date of Purchase	Return	% of Holdings
Visa	10/2008	572%	15.4%
Amazon	4/2012	310%	13.0%
Alphabet	10/2008	286%	10.6%
MasterCard	4/2011	315%	9.6%
Berkshire	1/2006	215%	9.4%
Facebook	11/2015	41%	8.4%
COSCO	1/2016	335%	8.4%
Schlumberger	1/2006	201%	5.4%
Philip Morris	1/2006	265%	5.4%
Microsoft	8/2015	32%	5.2%

These ten stocks amount to 74% of the portfolio. The other stocks equal 26% of the portfolio. Obviously, the top ten are carrying the entire portfolio. So far, the average holding period for these top stocks is six years—but no doubt it will be longer than that as we look forward. The average market cap for these top ten is

$227 billion. These are great companies who have become great investments.

Regarding the other stocks, does their holding size state that they are unlikely to become the top ten stocks? Well, the answer is yes, and no. Some of them will probably be held forever because they're just good enough. Some others could be every bit as good as the top ten and if we see an opportunity we'll add to these positions. The others are great companies, but if we could find substitutes with equal quality and better growth opportunity, we'd replace them.

When looking at the entire Smythe portfolio, one thing should stand out. With one minor exception, the stocks in the entire portfolio have no losses. In a vulnerable world like this, how is that possible? We believe that one of our greatest abilities is to admit when we're wrong and then…sell the losses. Having a portfolio with no losses is not because our selection process is perfect, it's because we sell those companies' stocks that don't meet our expectations.

There's one last point to be made throughout this seminar. I've preached the merits of high revenue growth because it generates high earnings growth. We stick to that. However, there are very few stocks who fit those criteria.

At some point, companies begin to mature. Revenues and earnings start to decelerate. Not go down, but grow at a slower rate year over year. As a company does this, it usually doesn't need to reinvest all of its cash flow. More often than not, these companies can't find anywhere to invest this cash.

As a best alternative, they begin or increase their stock repurchase program as well as their dividend payment. It can extend the attractiveness of their stock for years. It helps to look at a stock as though it is a teeter totter. On the left side is Revenues and Cashflows, the middle is earnings and the right side is stock repurchases and dividends. We concentrate on revenue and cash flow, reduce our interest in the middle and ignore the high repurchase of stock and high dividend paying stocks. When we do it correctly, we own it in the beginning, reduce it during the middle and be out of it by the end. One of our most difficult investment decisions is reducing the position during the middle. It's not only difficult to identify the middle; but, by then, the stock has achieved a huge gain which, when sold, will incur a large tax. We've got to be damn sure that we have a good substitute.

Additionally, our firm, deviated from the thinking of a large percentage of investors in the way we view dividends. When looking for common stocks, many investors look for dividends first. We, however, look for dividends last.

And when we do look, we're not concerned with what the dividend percentage is, we're interested in what the dividend rate of growth is. It will help you to remember this: dividends are taxed immediately, whereas stock appreciation, with planning, may never be taxed…as you will see.

As you look at these ten stocks you may have noticed that all of them are great companies. But some of them do not have great revenue or earning growth. So, what gives?

At the beginning of 2006, we owned four stocks which are currently in the portfolio: Berkshire, Philip Morris, Schlumberger, and Microsoft. In a few words, Berkshire is a cash flow company. It owns companies, stocks of companies, private equity, etc. The earnings that it generates are used mostly to buy more companies. It has no incentive stock options and doesn't pay a dividend. It is, in our opinion, the most tax efficient company that exists.

Philip Morris sells its product outside the U.S. Our clients have owned this stock for more than ten years and it has been a very successful investment. In the last few years, revenue and earnings growth have flattened and they have been hurt by the effects of a strong dollar. We have reduced our position in this stock.

Schlumberger caught us by surprise— it was more cyclical than expected and its earnings have declined. We continue to believe it is the best company in the energy world and that, in time, it's cyclicality will work to our advantage.

In the case of Microsoft, negative fundamentals caused us to sell the stock in 2007. Six years later we repurchased the stock as both revenues and earnings began to reaccelerate. This is the only stock in the last decade that we repurchased. Obviously, for us, it's a rarity.

From a fundamental standpoint, we have bought and sold about two stocks per year.

Summary

The Smythe Portfolio brings to the table things that the S&P 500 is unable to do:
- Premium Quality
- Faster Revenue, Cash Flow and Earnings Growth
- Ability to Sell Underperforming Stock
- Ability to Harvest

Chapter 26

Conclusion

The Returns of the S&P 500/Smythe Combo Compared to Alternative Investments

Take Away

The question to be asked is: how did the investment returns for the S&P 500, the Smythe Portfolio and the combo compare to alternative investments? This is not for a 25-year period. Rather, it is for the 10-year bear market cycle starting from the beginning of 2006 through 2015. If you want to know how a manager handled volatility…that's the time frame at which to look.

Verification

To prepare for this seminar, we went back to the beginning of 2006 and compiled returns for all the clients that were with us at that time. Usually, we ignore investment returns for 10 years. But this period of time produced one of the worst bear markets in history. The market peaked and then dropped 50% in 2008/9 and then recovered to new highs once again.

All of these clients owned equal proportions of the S&P 500 fund and the Smythe Portfolio. The S&P 500 compounded at 7.2% per year while the Smythe Portfolio compounded at 8.1%. When combined, the total compounded return was 7.6%.

It may not have occurred to you as you were looking at the Smythe Portfolio that it only owns stocks that were also owned by the S&P 500. Berkshire and Facebook are both middle top ten holdings and each account for 9.4% of Smythe's value and only 1.5% of S&P's value.

In essence, the combo portfolio is designed to maintain high diversification while increasing quality and investment performance. In fact, any change in volatility due to diversification was hardly noticeable, but the quality was enhanced and the annual rate of return increased from 7.2% to 7.6%.

The market at the beginning of the ten years was at an all-time high. Then it declined 50% and then it recovered and made new all-time highs before the end of the ten years: as always. During those 10 years, the annual pre-tax rate of return for the combined portfolio was 7.6%. But the real question is how did that return compare to the pre-tax rate of return achieved by alternative investments? The answers are listed in the accompanying table. They are not all of the alternatives that exist, but they are the major ones.

_____Average Us Stock Funds	_____European Funds
_____Large Cap Core Funds	_____Emerging Market Funds
_____Large Cap Growth Funds	_____Ten-Year Treasuries
_____Large Cap Value	_____Hedge Funds
_____Real Estate Funds	_____Balanced Funds
_____Precious Metals	_____Individual Investors

As you'll notice, there's a space next to each alternative. Would you mark the two or three that you wish you would have owned or think would have produced the best returns in the last ten years?

Alternative Investments, Pre-Tax Returns: 12/31/2005 through 12/31/2015	
	Yearly Return (%)
The S&P/Smythe Combo	7.6%
Average U.S. Stock Fund	5.6%
Large Cap Core Funds	5.7%
Large Cap Growth Funds	5.9%
Large Cap Value Funds	4.5%
Real Estate Funds	6.6%
Precious Metals	-4.6%
European Funds	4.1%
Emerging Markets	3.3%
10-Year Treasuries	5.5%
Hedge Funds	6.7%
Balanced Funds	5.3%
Individual Investors	3.5%
Combined Average Rate of Return:	4.4%

The point is this: Although our vision is for twenty-five years, and has an annual return range of 8% to 14%, we believe that it is every bit as important to understand that no matter what that return turns out to be, virtually all alternatives have been or may be about 2.5% less, per year. And let us not forget net after tax returns. Both the S&P 500 and the Smythe Portfolio are very tax efficient. The only tax paid by the S&P 500 is the dividend tax. And in the case of our Smythe Portfolio, because the dividends paid are only half of that of the S&P 500 (1% versus 2%) so are the dividend taxes. And because harvesting of losses eliminated capital gains taxes for the years of 2008, 2009, 2010, 2011 and most of 2012, it is questionable whether any of the investment alternatives had as low a ten-year capital gains rate as the Smythe Portfolio. In other words, no matter how you look at all the alternatives, pre-tax or after-tax, the rate of return for a quality investment—like the S&P 500 and Smythe Portfolio combo— is extremely hard to duplicate… let alone exceed.

To put this into perspective, let's examine how much profit would have been earned on $1,000,000 in the ten-year period.

In the case of the combo portfolio, which earned 7.6% per year, $1,000,000 would have grown to $2,080,200 for a profit of 1,080,200. The average alternative investment would have grown at 4.4% and produced a profit of $538,000.

And there's one more number to be considered: the individual investor who manages their own portfolio. Their 3.5% return produced a profit of $411,000.

Again,

	Profit	Total Portfolio
Combo S&P/Smythe Portfolio	$1,080,200	$2,080,200
Average Alternative Investment	$538,000	$1,538,000
Self-Managed Portfolio	$411,000	$1,411,000

The difference in profits is staggering. I'm not trying to insult you if you're an individual investor, but if you have any interest in managing your own money, you ought to know what you're up against.

There is one step left. It's called estate planning. Sometimes the planning is simple, with others it can be very complicated. But one component of estate planning can be managed long before you and your spouse pass on: it's capital gains taxes. On the day that you die (or your spouse), your cost basis on your investments is eliminated and a new cost basis takes its place. Usually its new cost basis is the date of death prices. The longer you hold your investments and the higher the price of those investments go up, the greater the amount of capital gains taxes are saved. Even in death, the name of the game is after tax returns.

Conclusion

For the taxable investor, whether you decide to manage your own portfolio or hire a manager to do it for you, may I suggest that you keep in mind the following principals of investing:

- Develop a permanent vision by understanding life expectancy and the magic of compounding.
- Know the expenses of investing before you invest.
- Learn both sides of asset allocation and make sure your behavior can support your allocation choice.
- Use the S&P 500 as your comparative standard.
- In the selection of stocks: quality will prevail. Seek out proprietary companies with sustainable revenues and cash flow goals.
- Keep your winners and sell your losers.
- In volatile markets, harvest losses as markets have always made higher highs; and understand that fear creates opportunity.
- As Monsieur St. Luc has said, like investing, "when planting the vine, …expect grapes to be harvested for forty years".

Remember this and thank you for your attendance.

Updated Through 2017

Two years ago, at Glacier Point, we presented our investment seminar which focused on the compounded annual rate of returns for the previous ten years for the S&P 500 and the S&P 500/Smythe Combo. The purpose for showing their returns was twofold. First was to show how each portfolio withstood the 2008/09 bear market. The second purpose was to show how investment returns of these two portfolios compared to all the major investment alternatives that existed in that period of time.

That was over two years ago. Today we are updating our time frame by extending our analysis from 10 years ago to 12 years; The beginning of 2006 through the end of 2017. But before we show that some of our investment principles have been reinforced in the last couple of years due to the following.

- 80% of all money managers, as well as individual investors, are value investors. Their primary approach to stock investing include a combination of low price earnings ratio accompanied by dividends paid.
- We have always known that 85% of all investors over time will underperform the S&P 500.

Is this a coincidence or did those two factors go hand in hand?

Growth has been leading the market for years while value investing just hasn't worked.

12 years ago is when we at Smythe identified a pattern of investing by most money managers which allowed us to benefit by their misplaced investing. We began to prioritize revenue growth as a leading indicator of future stock performance when combined with an analysis of a company's competitive advantage in the market. This provided the S&P 500/Smythe Combo's performance of $1,000,000 which is recoded below (after fees, before taxes).

2006	6.9%	$1,069,000
2007	17.3%	$1, 254, 000
2008	-32.8%	$843,000
2009	16.2%	$979,000
2010	13.3%	$1,109, 000
2011	4.4%	$1,158,000
2012	19.1%	$1,379,000
2013	32.8%	$1,831,000
2014	7.9%	$1,976,000
2015	8.5%	$2,144,000
2016	6.5%	$2,283,000
2017	29.9%	$3,004,000

For 12 years the S&P 500/Smythe Combo grew at 9.6% per year while the S&P 500 gained 8.3% per year. This is while the average alternative investment has produced an average return near 5.5% per year for the past 12 years.

The significance of compounding was discussed in several chapters but sometimes it's better understood by looking at raw numbers of a $1,000,000 investment.

	Annual Returns	Compounded Capital Growth
S&P 500/Smythe Combo	9.6%	$3,004,000
S&P 500 Index Fund	8.3%	$2,603,000
Average alternative investment	5.5%	$1,901,000

If these rates of return can be sustained for another 13 years we will have come within a whisker of attaining our 25 year goal of 10 million dollars.

	Annual Returns	Compounded Capital Growth
S&P 500/Smythe Combo	9.6%	$9,892,000
S&P 500 Index Fund	8.3%	$7,340,000
Average alternative investment	5.5%	$3,813,000

Everyone knows there are no guarantees in the stock market but permanent vision provides huge probabilities for the long-term investor. Make sure your portfolio takes advantage of that.